The Left Case for Brexit

The Left Case for Brexit

Reflections on the Current Crisis

Richard Tuck

polity

Copyright © Richard Tuck 2020

The right of Richard Tuck to be identified as Author of this Work has been asserted in accordance with the UK Copyright, Designs and Patents Act 1988.

First published in 2020 by Polity Press

Polity Press
65 Bridge Street
Cambridge CB2 1UR, UK

Polity Press
101 Station Landing
Suite 300
Medford, MA 02155, USA

ISBN-13: 978-1-5095-4227-7
ISBN-13: 978-1-5095-4228-4(pb)

A catalogue record for this book is available from the British Library.

Library of Congress Cataloging-in-Publication Data
Names: Tuck, Richard, 1949- author.
Title: The left case for Brexit : reflections on the current crisis / Richard Tuck.
Description: Bristol, UK ; Medford, MA : Polity, 2020. | Includes bibliographical references and index. | Summary: "Why opposing Brexit means opposing socialism and democracy"-- Provided by publisher.
Identifiers: LCCN 2019038607 (print) | LCCN 2019038608 (ebook) | ISBN 9781509542277 (hardback) | ISBN 9781509542284 (paperback) | ISBN 9781509542291 (epub)
Subjects: LCSH: European Union--Great Britain. | Socialism--Great Britain. | Democracy--Great Britain.
Classification: LCC HC240.25.G7 T83 2020 (print) | LCC HC240.25.G7 (ebook) | DDC 341.242/20941--dc23
LC record available at https://lccn.loc.gov/2019038607
LC ebook record available at https://lccn.loc.gov/2019038608

Typeset in 11 on 13pt Sabon by Fakenham Prepress Solutions, Fakenham, Norfolk NR21 8NL
Printed and bound in Great Britain by TJ International Limited

The publisher has used its best endeavours to ensure that the URLs for external websites referred to in this book are correct and active at the time of going to press. However, the publisher has no responsibility for the websites and can make no guarantee that a site will remain live or that the content is or will remain appropriate.

Every effort has been made to trace all copyright holders, but if any have been overlooked the publisher will be pleased to include any necessary credits in any subsequent reprint or edition.

For further information on Polity, visit our website:
politybooks.com

Contents

Contents

Preface

As the campaign began over the Brexit referendum which
was scheduled to take place on 23 June 2016, I found
myself increasingly troubled that there seemed to be few
people in the debate putting the old left-wing case against
Britain's membership of the European Union. I started
writing short essays for circulation among friends and
occasional publication in various online settings, and not
long before the vote I was asked to put some of these ideas
together into a piece for *Dissent*, which attracted quite a
lot of attention and encouraged me to develop the themes
further, and to reply to my critics. The Westminster-based
think-tank Policy Exchange invited me to set out my
thoughts in a lecture in July 2017, after the referendum
and the general election, and that enabled me to develop
my ideas further; I would like to thank Dean Godson,
its director, for his help and encouragement. I have also
continued to write short essays on the subject. This book
contains these pieces, in the order in which they were
written, to make it clear how I was responding to the
complicated twists and turns of British politics over the
last three years. Above all I would like to thank the friends
for whom they were first written: David Grewal, Daniela

Cammack, Alex Gourevitch, Jed Purdy, Chris Bickerton and Maurice Glasman. I would particularly like to thank Daniela Cammack for her help with this text. Many of the essays appeared on *The Full Brexit* website, the main organ of left-wing Brexiteers; I would like to thank the principal organisers of the site, Peter Ramsay, Lee Jones, Costas Lapavitsas, Martin Loughlin, Danny Nicol, Philip Cunliffe, Mary Davis, George Hoare, Anshu Srivastava and Aislinn Macklin-Doherty. Others have appeared on the *Briefings for Brexit* website; thanks to its organisers, Robert Tombs and Graham Gudgin.

16 April 2016

On 19 February 2016 David Cameron agreed with the other European leaders on the details of his renegotiation of the terms of membership for Britain in the European Union. The following day he announced that a referendum would be held on membership on 23 June. On 22 February the Commons debated the renegotiation deal, and the campaigning for the referendum began.

Do you remember David Cameron's renegotiation of the terms of Britain's membership of the EU? No, I thought not. The details of the negotiation have more or less disappeared without trace from the debate about Brexit, to be replaced by the apocalyptic scenarios of Project Fear, according to which Britain's exit from the EU will be catastrophic not merely for the British economy but for the entire Western World. At the very least Brexit (we are told) will carve a large hole in the European economy, but – even more urgently – it will apparently disrupt the entire current security system. When American politicians or generals (insofar as the categories are distinct) lecture the British on the need to stay in the EU, they are not doing so out of benevolence for Britain, nor do they even pretend to be doing so; they are doing it, they say, out of anxiety for the future of the post-war European order. The same is true of a certain kind of European politician, for whom the threat of terrorist attacks or Russian revanchism requires 'more Europe', and for whom the tearing apart of the EU would be a disaster.

But if we pause for a moment, we can see that there is something odd about this. Force yourself to remember the tedium of the renegotiation, and its footling outcomes: did it have the ring of a discussion conducted under the threat of the collapse of post-war Europe? Did it look like the really vital and urgent diplomatic engagements of the 1930s, in which it was obvious to everyone that major issues hung in the balance, or the similar negotiations of the Cold War? Either the EU representatives at Brussels in 2015–16 were extraordinarily insouciant about the implications of what they were doing, or they thought that Brexit was so unlikely (something which none of the polls, then or now, have supported, even if the balance of probability is for Remain) that it was not worth guarding against by offering politically plausible concessions, or they thought that a Brexit would not in fact be a disaster, and they could afford to run the risk of Britain walking away from the EU.

If they did not think any of these things, then there are only two explanations for the trivial character of the negotiations. One was that they were playing a game of chicken, in which they fully recognised the danger, but hoped to use fear of it as the key element in the negotiations, in order to force Britain into line. The EU of course has form in this regard: precisely this approach was used against Greece, as Yanis Varoufakis has testified. Rather than being offered some reasonable compromise, the Greek people and their government were led to believe that the choice was between exit from the euro – and even from the EU – and submission to the terms offered them. This was a manufactured choice, since they could relatively easily have been offered better terms; but the

Greeks' nerve failed, very reasonably, and they chose to swerve their car away from the centre of the highway.

The Greeks (to continue the analogy) were driving the equivalent of a Reliant Robin, which would have been no match for an armoured Mercedes even in a head-on collision, so the stakes were relatively low for the EU, as the international markets were repeatedly reminded. But with Brexit, the EU and the US are themselves now assuring us that the stakes are very high – though neither did so at all minatorily during the renegotiation. Sensible politicians do not play chicken in a high-stakes situation; neither the US nor the Soviet Union did so during the Cold War, except perhaps in the Cuban Missile Crisis – but that is no model for modern politics, and was anyway solved by a back-room deal rather than the submission of one side. Do we conclude that EU and State Department politicians are not sensible? Or do we conclude that they do not *really* believe what they say, since if they did, they would – according to their own lights – have been behaving in the most reckless fashion?

The other explanation for the absence of any sense of urgency and importance is that the EU representatives were terrified of offering anything more than trivial concessions, as doing so would have encouraged other countries to seek similar treatment, and the EU project would have begun to unravel. This may be right, but it does not bode well for the future of the project, and confirms that Britain would be best out of it. It reveals that the leaders of the EU do not themselves believe that there is general support for integration, and that the citizens of Europe, given half a chance, would opt for the kind of deal which British Eurosceptics want. Once again, then, the EU leaders are convicted of extraordinary recklessness in seeking to force European union upon unwilling populations by – in effect – a threat of expulsion levelled at one of the major member countries. How long can such a structure last?

22 April 2016

On 22 April President Barack Obama gave a press conference at the Foreign Office alongside David Cameron, in which he produced his famous remark that Britain would be 'at the back of the queue' when it came to a trade deal with the US. This remark was widely believed to have been drafted by the British government, given the fact that no American says 'queue' rather than 'line'! But Obama also said of the referendum that 'the outcome of that decision is a matter of deep interest to the United States because it affects our prospects as well. The United States wants a strong United Kingdom as a partner. And the United Kingdom is at its best when it's helping to lead a strong Europe. It leverages UK power to be part of the European Union.'

President Obama's intervention today in the Brexit debate tells us only one thing, but that is something of great significance. It is that President de Gaulle was right when in 1963 and 1967 he vetoed Britain's application to join the Common Market. In his public utterances on the issue, he stressed (as he said in a famous speech in 1963) that

> England in effect is insular, she is maritime, she is linked through her exchanges, her markets, her supply lines to the most diverse and often the most distant countries; she

pursues essentially industrial and commercial activities, and only slight agricultural ones. She has in all her doings very marked and very original habits and traditions.[1]

But the French press of the period, and private remarks by French politicians, repeatedly made explicit the specific anxiety which plainly guided de Gaulle's veto – that Britain would be 'America's Trojan Horse' in Europe. Within Britain, this has usually been seen as an example of French cultural anxiety; but with the crisis of Brexit on the horizon, the American foreign policy establishment is finally coming clean: they might talk about their general desire for a stable and united Europe, but in their eyes Britain's membership of the EU is and plainly always has been a means of planting a reliable agent of the United States in the heart of the organisation. The French fears of the 1960s were well founded in a quite definite sense, and it is highly likely that the French intelligence services, always preternaturally well informed, were aware at the time of this aspect of American foreign policy. And de Gaulle, with his intimate knowledge of Anglo-American relations as they had been forged during the Second World War, was in an especially good position to appreciate what British membership would mean.

Leaving aside the feelings of Continental politicians, now they have been told that what they always suspected was indeed the truth, and leaving aside the humiliation of British citizens on learning that their country has been acting as a secret agent for the US within the EU for fifty years, there is a serious question about what has now been revealed. The State Department's devotion to European union under all administrations should always have been more of a puzzle than it has normally appeared. There is much we do not know about its real motives, and about its attitude to British membership. For example, Richard Crossman, a member of Harold Wilson's Cabinet at the time of the renewed application in 1967, recorded in his diary that the Wilson government had turned to the Common Market only after an attempt to construct a North Atlantic free trade area between the US and Britain was rebuffed by the Johnson administration. Was this payback for Wilson's successful manoeuvrings which kept Britain out of the Vietnam War? Certainly, one would not have expected that America's most important military campaign since at least the Korean War would be fought without any British military involvement, while Australians and New Zealanders died on the battlefields of Vietnam (this should always be remembered by people who talk about Britain simply as America's poodle). Or was it already the policy of the State Department that Britain should be inserted into a Continental structure which was now being talked about quite openly in foreign ministries around the world as prospectively a political union? As Con O'Neill, the British representative to the EEC from 1963 to 1965 (and the man who led the successful negotiation to join), said in the characteristically flippant terms of the British diplomat:

> Mao Tse Tung declared that power grows out of the barrel of a gun. Professor Hallstein [the President of the Commission from 1958 to 1967] operates in a more sophisticated environment; but he has always declared he is in politics not business, and he may well believe that power grows out of the regulation price of Tilsit cheese or the price of a grain a hen needs to lay one egg. I think it does.[2]

There were – and still are – good reasons for the US to fear the EU rather than welcome it; beneath the veneer of Western solidarity there has always been a clear vein of anti-Americanism in the politics of the EU. During the Cold War this was obscured by the urgency of forming a united front against the Soviet Union, but even that requirement cut two ways: NATO and the military actions of the 1940s and 1950s such as the Berlin airlift were the most effective means of maintaining the Iron Curtain, and an independent Continental foreign policy led by France was not the most obvious pillar of Western security (and one should not forget the ever-present temptation of German unity bought by a promise of neutrality which the Soviet Union dangled in front of Germany throughout the Cold War, and which in a subtle fashion may turn out in the long run to be the bargain the Germans accepted). Nowadays, one would have thought that any objective analysis of a traditional kind would conclude that the EU was potentially more of a risk to the US than to Russia: it is the EU which is economically successful, which can interfere with American companies in one of their largest markets, and which can increasingly play an independent – and, as it turns out, often catastrophic – role in foreign affairs, as in the disastrous Libyan adventure cooked up by Britain and France, who seem to see themselves as the basis of a kind of EU military force. But America's fears of the EU have been assuaged over the years by Britain's presence; the extraordinary level of integration in foreign policy between the two countries has been a guarantee that the EU will not develop in an openly hostile way.

In the days before the radical extension of qualified majority voting to most important matters that come before the EU Council of Ministers, Britain's role as a Trojan Horse was very straightforward, since it could veto measures that it – or the State Department – opposed. That is no longer the case, as the demand for Brexit within Britain testifies; the central fear of the advocates of Brexit is after all that Britain, with its special interests which are seldom shared by other countries within the EU, will be consistently outvoted – it has been in the minority more than any other state in the last decade, and that is only likely to get worse. Most opponents of the EU in Britain would be mollified by a return to the voting arrangements which were in place when Britain joined. But the State Department does not yet appear to have drawn the obvious conclusion, which is that Britain will not be an especially effective Trojan Horse in the future. Even its military role, as it has come increasingly under the spell of French military revanchism, will be far less reliable as a means of projecting American influence inside Europe. At the extreme, the Horse may be turned against the Greeks themselves, and that prospect ought to keep undersecretaries of state awake at night far more than the prospect of Brexit. The very reasons which drive the campaign for Brexit should – if the State Department were thinking clearly – make it very unconfident that the old order will be maintained even if Britain stays in the EU, and very fearful of what may happen if the existing project simply limps forward for another generation or more. One might even say that the last couple of decades have seen an historic defeat for American foreign policy; the European settlement in which Britain functioned as its arm within the EU was gradually transformed in the course of a subterranean diplomatic struggle into a new arrangement in which Britain cannot play the role assigned to it. Overconfident as ever, the British Foreign Office has clearly continued to pretend to the US that it holds the key to Europe; the snag is that one day the State Department will discover that the locks have been changed.

There are wider issues which the question of America's attitude to Britain and the EU raises. Secrecy has always been part of the business of international affairs, with negotiations conducted entirely in private, and possibly without the agreements which are made ever becoming fully public. In the past there were secret treaties (such as Charles II's infamous Treaty of Dover, which in retrospect bears some similarities to the EU treaties!), and though they have largely vanished, the world of diplomacy still operates with a far higher level of concealment and subterfuge than would ever be acceptable in domestic politics. Traditionally, citizens have accepted this: the ambassador, sent to lie abroad for the good of his country, did not usually threaten the internal political structures of his nation, and if he did he would be summarily dismissed or prosecuted. One of the deep problems of the modern international order, of which the EU is the most extreme example, is that this is no longer the case. International agreements bite deep into the internal organs of states, but they are arrived at by the same opaque processes by which they have always been handled. Given the traditional division between executive and legislative, moreover, and the fact that foreign affairs are usually the special province of the executive, this feature of the modern world has handed enormous new powers to governments. The American senators who blocked the US membership of the League of Nations may have known (at some subconscious level) what they were doing – just as Weber said the reactionary opponents of civil service reform in nineteenth-century America knew what they were doing when they resisted the move to a modern bureaucracy. The fact that we do not really know exactly *why* Britain is in the EU, and the smell of secrecy which hangs over both the history of its accession and the recent diplomacy to keep it in the EU, are among the principal reasons for wishing to get out.

16 May 2016

By mid-May it was becoming likely that Hillary Clinton would win the Democrats' nomination for President, but Bernie Sanders' supporters still had some reason for hope. In an NBC/Wall Street Journal poll, 53% of respondents said they would vote for Sanders if Trump were the Republican nominee, and only 39% for Trump, whereas Clinton and Trump were in a dead heat ...

One of the curious ways in which British and American politics continue to run parallel with one another – think Thatcher/Reagan and Clinton/Blair – is that in both countries at the moment class war, and class contempt, have unexpectedly reappeared. In both countries, moreover, one of the key issues has been international trade: in the US the argument is over the Trans-Pacific Partnership (TPP) and in the UK the argument is over Brexit. But on both sides of the Atlantic, trade has come to stand in for a much wider range of threats which the old working class faces. The difference between the two countries, however, is that in America the Left has understood this and – to a degree – has been able genuinely to speak to it, while in Britain the Left has remained imprisoned in the mindset of the Clinton/Blair years, however much it might ostensibly deny it.

The degree to which commentators in this new world feel able to express their contempt for the pathetic losers stranded by the glorious capitalism of the recent past is quite astonishing. From the United States comes the infamous article by Kevin D. Williamson from the *National Review* in March 2016 about Garbutt, a decaying industrial town in upstate New York:

> The truth about these dysfunctional, downscale communities is that they deserve to die. Economically, they are negative assets. Morally, they are indefensible. The white American under-class is in thrall to a vicious, selfish culture whose main products are misery and used heroin needles. Donald Trump's speeches make them feel good. So does OxyContin. What they need isn't analgesics, literal or political. They need real opportunity, which means that they need real change, which means that they need U-Haul. If you want to live, get out of Garbutt...[3]

But that can be exactly matched by a column in the London *Times* eighteen months earlier by the socially liberal Conservative Matthew Parris writing about a by-election in Clacton-on-Sea, a decaying seaside town in Essex. UKIP duly went on to win the seat.

> [U]nderstand that Clacton-on-Sea is going nowhere. Its voters are going nowhere, it's rather sad, and there's nothing more to say. This is Britain on crutches. This is tracksuit-and-trainers Britain, tattoo-parlour Britain, all-our-yesterdays Britain.
>
> So of course Ukip will do well in the by-election ...
>
> If you want to win Cambridge you may have to let go of Clacton.
>
> From the train leaving Stratford at platform 10a, you can see Canary Wharf [where many of the biggest banks in London are based], humming with a sense of the possible. You must turn your back on that if you want to go to Clacton. I don't, and the Tories shouldn't ...[4]

As Parris's invective testifies, in Britain UKIP, whose raison d'être since its foundation in 1993 has been to get Britain out of the EU, is the movement which has managed to reach these voters, and indeed in many northern towns, and now South Wales, has managed to peel them away from their traditional Labour loyalties. UKIP is universally despised by the liberal intelligentsia, and in this respect as in many others it resembles the Trump wing of the Republican Party; though since it operates outside the traditional party structures it has very little chance of achieving any real political break-through in ordinary elections. But in the current Brexit campaign it is yoked in a somewhat uneasy fashion to quite prominent figures from the Conservative Party, with the campaign as a whole coming to look rather more like an insurgency within the mainstream right-wing party – and with the one of the main leaders of the campaign, the former Mayor of London Boris Johnson, as many commentators have pointed out, strangely resembling Trump, including his distinctive hairstyle, his reputation made partly through appearances on TV shows, and a history of womanising. There are important differences, though: Johnson as Mayor presided enthusiastically and with great popularity over what must be the most culturally mixed city on the planet, and it is hard to imagine a President Trump addressing Congress in Latin, as Johnson on occasion addressed the London Assembly. He is also genuinely funny and charming, in a way Trump will never be. His success as Mayor in fact illustrates an important truth about Brexit (which may not have a parallel in the US): there is little enthusiasm for the EU among the large non-European population of the capital, and of the country as a whole. South Asians, for example, understand that EU immigration policies will inevitably make it harder for people like them to come to Britain in the future.

Nevertheless, the similarities between the electorate which has been looking to Trump and Sanders as its

defenders against a globalising, capitalistic and merito-
cratic elite (with this last trait perhaps being the most
significant, as Thomas Frank pointed out in a brilliant
book[5]), and the electorate which is currently looking
to a Brexit, are very striking. But as I said, there is one
major difference: there is no British Bernie Sanders. For a
while it looked as if the new leader of the Labour Party,
Jeremy Corbyn, might play the role; he even has a long
history of opposition to the EU and voted against it in the
last referendum. But he has disappointed almost all his
followers, and has allowed himself to be captured by the
pro-EU forces in his party. The Labour figures associated
with Brexit have failed to catch the public's eye, and the
result is that Brexit is seen as largely a movement within
the Conservatives. And yet, as the American primaries
have shown, there is a real left-wing case to be made
for the necessity of giving this deracinated working-class
electorate a real voice of the traditional kind, and the one
American politician who has seen this has so far reaped
unexpectedly great rewards. But in Britain almost all my
friends say that they cannot support Brexit because of the
political and cultural identities of the leaders of the Brexit
campaign, even though most of them simultaneously voice
scepticism about the EU, and even though most of them
are long-range enthusiasts for Sanders.

Why is there no Sanders campaigning for Brexit?
Why in a country without a major modern tradition of
socialism is a self-described socialist doing so well, while
in a country with a long-standing supposedly socialist
party no one is willing to step up and fight this cause? The
last time the question was put to the vote, heavyweight
figures from Labour campaigned against the Common
Market, including the man now seen as in some sense the
model for Corbyn, Tony Benn. But there is no one like
that within the party today. Some rather feeble gestures
are currently being made towards the old working-class
English electorate: Tristram Hunt, the former Shadow
Secretary of State for Education (and, oddly enough, a

biographer of Engels), has recently urged his party not to neglect it, and allow it to fall into the hands of UKIP. But Hunt and the figures like him in the party can offer nothing any more which that electorate wants: it has correctly perceived that the only kinds of change which will make a real difference to it are precisely those which are precluded by Britain's membership of the EU, not to mention by all the structures (such as an independent central bank) put in place by the last Labour government. Labour politicians still believe that political science – the technical organisation of a party – can win back its lost ground; but as Hillary Clinton is discovering, only political theory can do that.

So the question remains: why no British Sanders? One explanation might be the institutional difference between American and English politics: it is hard to make the kind of run outside conventional party structures which both Trump and Sanders have managed. But this is not a satisfactory explanation, since the Brexit campaign offers exactly this kind of opportunity, and Johnson, who is not exactly a conventional party figure, has duly seized it. I think the true explanation, unfortunately, is Britain's membership of the EU itself. Resisting the TPP, or even annulling NAFTA, are simple tasks compared with the difficulties of extracting Britain from the EU. Faced with that, a generation of Labour politicians have lost their nerve. It then becomes a vicious circle as, with no one on the Left willing to defend Brexit, the cause looks as if it is (to put it in American terms) purely Trump – and then the politicians, and most party members, feel ashamed at being associated with it. Consequently there is no way of recovering Labour's lost working-class support: as in Scotland, the party drank from the poisoned chalice of the EU, and it may be too late to find the antidote.

6 June 2016:
The Left Case for Brexit

On 6 June 2016 I published an article entitled 'The Left Case for Brexit' in the online edition of Dissent *magazine,[6] which attracted a great deal of attention on both sides of the Atlantic, including a recommendation by Charles Moore in* The Spectator *of 18 June. The article was based on some posts I had written during the previous month, including one which responded to an article by Yanis Varoufakis published on 5 April in* The Guardian *containing an extract from his new book,* And the Weak Suffer What They Must, *which was published the same week. Varoufakis ended his article by saying that, 'Just like in the early 1930s, Britain and Greece cannot escape Europe by building a mental or legislative wall behind which to hide. Either we band together to democratise – or we suffer the consequences of a pan-European nightmare that no border can keep out.' This is an edited version of the article, incorporating some more of those earlier posts.*

On the question of whether Britain should leave the European Union, the British Left has been nearly uniform in supporting 'Remain'. This option seems especially attractive since those on the Right advocating 'Leave' range from open racists concerned with the recent growth of immigration to romantic global free-marketeers. For entirely understandable cultural and political reasons, the Left has not wished to be associated with that crowd. But in supporting 'Remain', the Left is making a profound mistake, one capable of destroying its future, whether Britain is in or out of the EU.

There are several flaws in the case made by Left advocates of Remain; here I want to consider three in particular. First is the idea, fostered especially by the dynamic Greek former finance minister, Yanis Varoufakis, that Left politics today can only be advanced by concerted action within the EU. As I will argue, that is a fantasy, and by adhering to it the British Left is likely to undermine itself seriously – as the Greek Left may already be doing.

Next is the claim that Brexit would hasten the break-up of the United Kingdom, and consequently (for long-standing reasons of electoral demography) spell doom for Labour as a party of government. I argue that the opposite is the case: Brexit may well be the only thing that could hold the UK together and offer Labour the opportunity to rebuild on a national basis.

Last is the assumption, which seems to underlie much pro-Remain thinking on the Left, that the EU is fundamentally different from the multinational trade agreements – most recently the Transatlantic Trade and Investment Partnership (TTIP) and the TPP – that are reshaping the global economic order. While many leftists have clear and well-thought-out arguments against such trade 'partnerships', they give their unconsidered support to the EU, though it suffers from all the same failings and more.

As a consequence of these mistakes, the British Left risks throwing away the one institution which it has, historically, been able to use effectively – the democratic state – in favour of a constitutional order tailor-made for the interests of global capitalism and managerial politics. As the jurisprudence of the EU has developed, it has consistently undermined standard Left policies such as state aid to industries and nationalisation. Constitutional structures that are largely outside the reach of citizens have, in the modern world, tended almost invariably to block the kind of radical policies that the Left has traditionally believed in. The central fact about the EU, which the British governing class has never really got its head around, is that it creates a written constitution and ancillary juridical structures that are extremely hard to alter. Neither British politicians nor the British electorate are used to this, since Britain has never had such a thing, and they are treating the referendum as if it were a general election campaign, with short-term victories that could be reversed in a few years, rather than something with the long-term implications of the votes in 1788 on the American Constitution.

I

Yanis Varoufakis is one of the most significant left-wing politicians in Europe. As someone who witnessed one of its major crises from within, he speaks with authority about the character of the EU project. His accounts of the discussions in the councils of Europe about the euro crisis, featuring ignorant and preening finance ministers bent almost exclusively on the exercise of power, are a graphic illustration of what actually happens within the EU.

Varoufakis is also important because despite his first-hand experience of the limits of the EU, he believes it can be reformed. More than that, he hopes that a pan-European Left will be revived through the institutions of the EU, and that hope is repeatedly echoed by pro-EU figures within the British Labour Party. But it would be a profound mistake for the British Left to follow Varoufakis's loyalty to the European project. To see why, we should go back to the theorist with whom Varoufakis himself continues to identify: the founding father of the European Left, Karl Marx.

One of Marx's most striking insights was the observation that the various constitutions of the French Republics, and their imitations in other Continental states, were deliberately designed to obstruct progress towards genuine democracy. Though the French Revolution had introduced universal suffrage, its significance was immediately undermined by the Declaration of the Rights of Man and by constitutional structures that precluded the kind of social transformation that the Revolution's radicals wanted. Marx emphasised this repeatedly in his writings of the 1840s, and the failure of the revolutions of 1848 and the restoration of the constitutional orders in Europe only confirmed his judgment. Accordingly, Marx felt, only a total revolution would be able to overturn the 'bourgeois' liberal economic and political constitutions that stood in the way of substantive social change.

But Marx, and still more Engels, thought England was different. The House of Commons was unconstrained by the kind of constitutional apparatus seen on the Continent, since Parliament was (famously) 'omnicompetent' and the Lords and the monarchy were largely irrelevant. Marx and Engels concluded that once the English working class got the vote, it would be able to use the House of Commons to achieve its political and economic goals peacefully. The accidents of history that had delivered this exceptional institution meant that revolution ought not to be necessary for the kind of social transformation Marx and Engels had in mind.

The early members of the Labour Party in England (who were more Marxist than their successors cared to admit) understood this, and believed that a properly organised working class, using representation in the House of Commons as its vehicle, could institute radical economic and social change. And compared with the life of the working class in the nineteenth century, working-class life after the growth of Labour vindicated their confidence. Indeed, the greatest achievement of the Labour Party, the creation of the National Health Service, would have been impossible in a country with strong constitutional constraints on the legislature, since it required the large-scale expropriation of private property in the shape of the old endowed hospitals. That is a major reason why so few countries have adopted the NHS model: in most of them it would have been illegal, just as similar proposals would be illegal in the EU today.

In the 1980s, however, demoralised Labour politicians began to seek the shelter of Continental-style constitutional structures. The most important and obvious of these structures is the EU, which functions for the internal politics of its member states exactly like the bourgeois constitutions of the mid-nineteenth century, though the Blair government introduced various other checks on the House of Commons such as a newly energised and apparently more independent 'Supreme Court', and an independent central bank.

The loss of faith in the advancement of left-wing politics through the ballot box may partly be explained by the success of Thatcher, though I would be more inclined to say that it was the other way round, and that Thatcher was victorious over a Labour Party many of whose most important figures had already lost confidence in traditional electoral politics and whose hearts were not really in the struggle against her. The defection of leading members of the party to the new Social Democrats in 1981, largely on the issue of Europe, symbolises this. It is a mistake to think that Thatcher's victory in 1979 was necessarily the beginning of the long period of Tory government which it turned out to be: the Labour Party split with astonishing rapidity, only two years after Thatcher's first election, and before the landslide of her second election in 1983. Labour politicians had already succumbed to the temptation to use an external order to put in place left-wing policies *before* Thatcher began to roll back the achievements of the Left (and in the case of Roy Jenkins, there was also the allure of personal power within the external order). This was precisely the temptation which Jacques Delors dangled in front of the TUC in his famous speech in 1988, and which brought the rest of the Labour Party round to the same position on the EU which the Social Democrats had espoused.

But like all temptations of this kind, it was not what it seemed. The same structures which Delors promised to use in the interests of the working class turned out by the time of the financial crash in 2007–8 to have been used instead to push through a neoliberal economic and social agenda. This would not have surprised Marx: as he understood, this is really the default position of such structures, since their whole point is and always has been to repress what Continental politicians call with disdain 'populism' – that is, democracy. As a Marxist, and given his own bruising encounters with EU institutions, Varoufakis should perhaps see this better than anyone. But despite fiercely criticising the way the EU handled the Greek crisis, Varoufakis has remained loyal to the idea that left-wing politics can be pushed through using EU institutions, if only the parties of the Left across Europe can properly coordinate their activities.

History would suggest that this is a vain hope. Even if Europe's Left parties do succeed in forging a common programme, the EU is not the kind of political entity whose approach to the world can be altered by popular politics. Popular politics is precisely what the EU was designed to obstruct. Like independent central banks and constitutional courts, its institutions are essentially technocratic. Technocracy is not (as some like to pretend) a neutral or rational system of government. Instead, it confers immense power on culturally select bodies whose prejudices will be those of the class their members are drawn from.

Varoufakis believes that the EU may change, and many in the British Labour Party agree. But the kind of shift in European politics that Varoufakis and others want to see is simply not possible within the present structures of the EU: it would require sweeping institutional change of a kind nowhere on the agenda. Without that, like the Labour Party in Britain, the Left in Europe is reliant purely on an article of faith – a conviction that the Left must prevail, even in the face of all the constraints imposed on popular sovereignty by the EU.

The British governing class in the late twentieth century threw away the most valuable institution it had inherited, an institution whose preservation was the most obvious imperative for their predecessors: a House of Commons that was not constrained by a constitution. A vote to stay within the EU will render their casual trashing of it irrevocable, and end any hope of genuinely Left politics in the UK.

II

If these fundamental considerations were not enough to persuade the Left to vote to leave the EU, pragmatic politics should do so. The Labour Party since Blair has made a fundamental misjudgment about how to gain power, a misjudgment intimately related to its stance on the EU: this is its misunderstanding of Scottish politics.

It is now clear that the Labour Party, in the shape in which it has existed for upwards of a century, is dead. The loss of Scotland, as many commentators have observed, renders it virtually impossible that the Labour Party will rule again in a united kingdom; and since England has been a fundamentally Tory country since the seventeenth century, and shows no sign of becoming markedly less so, it is hard to see anything like the old Labour Party taking power in England alone. Something along these lines has been the obvious prize dangling in front of the Tory Party since Scottish nationalism became a serious political force, and David Cameron – whether through extraordinary luck or extraordinarily good judgment – has seized the prize without (so far) having to break up the United Kingdom in order to do so. In the aftermath of the debacle of the 2015 general election people both inside and outside the Labour Party have been quick to blame its failure on its rotten boroughs and sectarian politics in the West of Scotland, with long-festering resentments and disillusionments finally coming to the surface. But there is a much more fundamental reason why Labour sooner or later had to fail in Scotland.

Modern Scottish nationalism is essentially the working out within Britain of the logic of the EU. Scotland joined the Union in 1707 explicitly to enjoy an economic union with a large market and a global trading power, and there is no need for it to stay within the old union when a new one beckons; why have an intermediate level of politics in Westminster when everything can be much more easily decided directly between Edinburgh and Brussels? To see this, one need only consider whether Scottish nationalism could be a credible movement if the EU did not exist. The EU's institutions guarantee Scotland virtually the same freedoms of trade and movement with England which the 1707 Union provided; the only missing element (as the equivocation of the referendum campaign demonstrated) is a common currency, but the EU offers some security to an independent Scotland even in this area, at least as compared with the risks of a wholly independent and wholly Scottish currency, the failure of which was a principal reason for the British Union.

Indeed, one does not have to imagine this: one only has to think back (if one is old enough, as I am) to the days before Britain joined the Common Market, when Scottish nationalism was largely a joke, and its supporters' principal activity was moving the Welcome to Scotland sign from one side of Berwick-upon-Tweed to the other. Even after Britain's accession, as long as the Common Market appeared to be merely a somewhat loose trading arrangement it played no part in Scottish nationalism – indeed, the SNP had violently opposed the accession. But once the Common Market began to take its current shape, the power of European integration to advance its cause began to dawn on the SNP, and as soon as it switched to an enthusiastically pro-European position in the 1980s its electoral fortunes began to improve.

There is little to set against the power of this logic. The ties of sentiment between Scotland and England can be maintained if both countries are united with one another *via* the EU as easily as in a United Kingdom; witness the ways in which strong ties continued between England and Ireland despite their separation since 1921, as long as freedom of movement and a high degree of economic integration were guaranteed. Enemies of Scottish nationalism often deny that an independent Scotland would be part of the EU, but no one is convinced: given the character and ambitions of the EU, is it at all plausible that an independent Scotland would be left outside while England stayed within? It would surely become a second Ireland, welcomed as an independent nation at Brussels, whatever the Spaniards (in particular) might say or do.

These obvious thoughts do not need to have been in the forefront of the minds of the almost half of the Scottish electorate who voted for independence in the referendum, though they have certainly been in the forefront of the minds of the SNP leaders; it is enough that the EU is simply now part of the necessary background to any discussion about the separation of the two countries, and as its clear logic works its way to a conclusion it is hard to see the old United Kingdom surviving. Even if it does, in some precarious fashion, the plausibility of Scottish independence in this context will remain, and will continue to attract large numbers of voters to the SNP and away from Labour.

The Labour Party should have remembered that more than the other parties it was a creature of the United Kingdom; it only came into being towards the end of the UK's most powerful century, and from the start it was heavily represented in all four nations. It even organised in Ireland prior to 1913, when (in an ominous precedent for the current Labour Party) it withdrew in the face of Irish Home Rule, creating in its place a separate but affiliated Irish Labour Party which has continued as a party in the Republic until the present day. From this perspective, the carelessness with which Blair approached the twin questions of Scottish devolution and European integration was suicidal for his party.

It remains one of the great oddities of modern British history that the powerful voices within the Labour Party in the Wilson and Callaghan years opposing membership of the Common Market were so easily silenced after the party's defeat in 1983 (when its manifesto had included a pledge to withdraw from the EEC), and that the Conservatives and Labour so swiftly swapped places on this issue: in many ways the objective interests of the two parties remained what they had been in the 1970s, and the instinctive suspicion of European integration felt by many people in the Labour Party corresponded to the structural position of the party in British electoral politics. This is leaving to one side, of course, the well-founded character of the suspicion that European integration would prove disastrous for the cause of traditional socialism, as European history over the last two decades has so amply demonstrated. Both democracy and socialism require a state, and the EU looks increasingly as if it will offer its residents something far short of a democratic state at the supra-national level, but powerful enough to destroy the old democracies at a national level, in the process handing capitalism a freedom it has always desired.

Is there any rowing back from this disaster? All that the current leaders of the Labour Party offer is an act of will: a resolution that there *must* be a Labour government once again in the UK. But none of them are providing any plausible analysis of how such a thing can be achieved. At the moment it looks as if Cameron may succeed in setting the capstone on his historic defeat of the Labour Party by engineering a victory in a referendum on Britain's continued membership of the EU, supported in doing so by the very Labour politicians whose future the EU is destroying. Such a framework will continue to facilitate Scottish independence and prevent a United Kingdom

Labour Party from effectively rebuilding in Scotland. But suppose that the vote in the referendum goes in favour of leaving the EU; what then? The SNP has moved quickly to declare that it will not be bound by such a result if Scotland votes to stay in the EU, and Nicola Sturgeon has attempted to argue that each constituent nation would have to be in favour of leaving before the UK as a whole could leave. This illustrates the extreme importance of this issue for the future of Scottish nationalism, and the judgment of the SNP leaders themselves that continued British membership of the EU offers the best route to independence. But what would actually happen depends on the nature of a post-referendum settlement with the EU, and no one has any idea what that might look like; indeed, the pro-EU camp will make it their prime objective to keep any possible post-Brexit settlement completely unclear, as the pro-Unionists did in the Scottish referendum.

It should be said that the most likely arrangements following Brexit bode only a little better for the future of the United Kingdom than does continued membership of the EU. It is extremely unlikely that Brexit would leave the UK standing in the same relationship to the EU as (say) Canada does; that is, as a wholly foreign country. But if that were to be the case, and Scotland were subsequently to leave the UK and join the EU, there would be a completely unprecedented situation, since for the first time in post-medieval history there would be real barriers to trade and the movement of population within the islands of Ireland and Britain. Even after Irish independence, as I said, there was continued integration of the two populations and to all intents and purposes of the two economies, with Ireland recognising in 1973 that if the UK were to join the Common Market it would have to follow suit. Already there are some voices being raised in Ireland suggesting that a Brexit might entail an Irish exit as well, and a break with the EU of this radical kind would certainly cause major problems for both Ireland

and an independent Scotland – so great, indeed, that it would probably deter Scottish voters from supporting independence.

But this is extremely unlikely as a post-Brexit scenario. Much more likely is that Britain would enjoy something like the relationship with the EU which Norway has; this is indeed the option often cited by opponents of British membership. The relevance of this to Scottish nationalism is that Norway has two kinds of relationship to the EU; one is its membership of the European Economic Area, along with Iceland (and Lichtenstein), but the other is its continued membership, also along with Iceland, of the Nordic Passport Union. The Nordic Passport Union guarantees free movement of people and an integrated labour market among the Scandinavian countries (which is why both Iceland and Norway have to belong to Schengen – just as the Irish, with in effect a passport union with the UK, cannot belong to Schengen as long as the UK stays outside). This would indeed be the obvious model for an England outside the EU but still integrated with the other two insular countries inside it.

But equally obviously such a model would do little to hold back Scottish nationalism: if Denmark can be in the EU but Norway outside it, why cannot Scotland, and Ireland, be inside the EU and England outside it? So even if the vote in the referendum were to be in favour of exit, at least in England, the most likely and attractive post-referendum settlement would not stop the steady advance of Scotland towards independence, and with it the slow death of the Labour Party. There may now simply be no undoing the mistakes which the party made under Kinnock and Blair. But if the Labour Party cares at all about the future of its role in a united kingdom, the worst thing it can do is oppose Brexit: Brexit offers the only prospect, however slight it may be, of preserving the United Kingdom and rebuilding a British Labour Party.

III

One of the odd things about British leftists' support of the EU is that when they are invited to support a very similar institution with a different set of members, they resolutely refuse to do so. Many people on the Left now oppose both the TPP and the TTIP. They do so partly for economic reasons. But much of the opposition to these trade agreements is based on their political implications, and in particular the regulatory structures which they put in place and impose on individual states. These treaties are not old-fashioned trade agreements to lower tariffs. Instead, they attempt to construct coordinated regulatory structures in a wide variety of areas, ranging from workers' rights to industrial policy and environmental regulations. Such provisions clearly intrude on areas of national life that in the past were presumed to be the preserve of national governments. Furthermore, the treaties create mechanisms for so-called Investor–State Dispute Settlement (ISDS) which amount to the creation of supranational courts, ruling in accordance with loose principles and free from appellate scrutiny.

Liberal defenders of global capitalism led by President Obama like to stress the fact that the treaties enshrine workers' rights and gender equality, and they imply that the other provisions are necessary to enforce these rights and to prevent states from restricting free trade through such means as the manipulation of labour laws and health and safety regulations. But the fundamental fact is that supranational intervention on behalf of left-wing causes is bundled together with intervention on behalf of modern global capitalism, and it is not difficult to see which type of intervention will have – and is intended to have – the most lasting impact.

Everything I have just said is commonplace in discussions on the Left across Europe. But many British leftists do not see that these points also apply to the European

Union. The EU anticipated both this kind of bundling of left-wing with right-wing promises and the assumption that modern free trade requires a supranational structure with powers to intervene in the internal life of the member states. Because there are so many ways in which regulatory hurdles can be erected to restrict trade, it is argued, regulation has to be managed at a supra-national level. And like the partnerships, in practice the EU subordinates its concern with workers' rights to its concern to maintain the freedom of companies to shop around within the EU for the weakest regimes of labour protection. To see that, one need only look at European Court of Justice judgments concerning transna-tional labour disputes within the EU, which the European Trade Union Confederation has described as confirming 'a hierarchy of norms ... with market freedoms highest in the hierarchy, and collective bargaining and action in second place'.[7]

It is the Right that ought to applaud this kind of structure, and the Left that ought to be hostile – this is the paradox at the heart of the current British argument about EU membership. Free trade is never the unalloyed good to everyone which is promised: everything depends on the political power of the various groups concerned, something the Left has usually understood, and which the renascent US Left has rediscovered. Anxiety about the TTIP in Britain and the rest of Europe is well judged; but there is no point in resisting the TTIP, or even employing European political institutions to prevent the EU signing up to it, if we remain within the EU. Everything that is objectionable to the Left about these trade partnerships, with the single exception of the fact that the United States is involved, should be objectionable to the Left when it comes to the EU. This was what the original opponents of the Common Market in the Labour Party understood in 1975, and time has merely proven them correct.

IV

It is hard to avoid the conclusion that the Left's natural position should still be one of opposition to the EU. Why is this message proving so hard to get across? One reason is the fact that many centres of the Left, such as universities, have done very well financially out of the EU. Overall, Britain contributes more to the EU budget than it receives back, but it has proven easier for many academic institutions to negotiate grants from the EU than from the UK government. But this is scarcely a good argument: first, those institutions should not be protected from democratic politics, particularly as far and away the bulk of their funding still comes from the UK taxpayer; and second, no one knows how negotiations would go in the absence of EU largesse. No government, aware that universities can at the moment get funding from the EU, will offer money of its own, but that does not mean it would not do so if that funding were withdrawn.

The most powerful reason, I think, is cultural and political hostility to the supporters of Brexit, and in particular to their stance on immigration, and a fear of what happens in general if they win. But this fear is self-reinforcing. The Left is frightened because it has chosen to abandon the field to its enemies, rather than because of any necessary cleavage between Left and Right on the EU. One can put this point in a more vivid way by asking, why is there no British Bernie Sanders? Sanders has shown that the alienated working-class vote can still be won by left-wing policies, particularly on global trade, and need not be abandoned to the radical Right. But the British Left cannot make that move, despite a degree of windy rhetoric. And the reason it cannot is that its power to propose genuinely left-wing policies has been severely circumscribed by the EU.

The way for the Left to address the immigration debate is to understand that immigration is to many people only the most vivid and proximate sign of a more general loss of political power. Nothing will answer those people's concerns unless they can be told that decisions about immigration policy are going to be in the hands of the British electorate, like all decisions of major importance. The debate can then begin over what kind of immigration policy the Left should support, and whether (like the present system) it should in effect give priority to white Europeans over the older classes of immigrants in Britain, predominantly South Asian, who wish to unite families and move easily between Britain and South Asia. The Left should also appreciate that the traditional heart of modern left-wing politics, a planned welfare state, is rendered virtually impossible if Britain stays in the EU, since no one will have any idea of the population numbers in the UK even in the near future. This is an illustration of the way the free movement of people in the EU, as well as of goods and capital, almost necessarily entrenches markets rather than collective planning.

Many of my English friends on the Left reply to these arguments with despair: nothing can now be done to change the situation, the forces of globalisation are too strong, the political culture of Britain is too conservative. Membership of the EU offers shelter, despite its patent lack of democracy and its basic sympathy with capitalism. But this is to rationalise defeat. There have been times in living memory when the Left in Britain could assert itself successfully, but those were times when it understood the nature of Britain's political structures and could use them. The lack of political possibilities perceived by so many people today is the result of quite specific decisions, above all to enter the EU, and I see no reason why reversing that decision would not open up real possibilities for the Left in Britain again.

9 June 2016

So far, most of the responses to my 'Left Case for Brexit' have fallen into three groups. The first expresses the simple and understandable fear that a Brexit will hand power in Britain to the people who have been most vocal in its support, and they do not include many figures on the Left. Brexit would therefore represent an historic defeat for the Left in Britain. The point of my article, however, is that there has always been a Left case for Brexit, and that abandoning the field to the Right was the historic mistake which there should be some attempt, even at this late stage, to reverse. Continuing to oppose Brexit simply means doubling down on this mistake. Moreover, the defeat of the Left after Brexit is inevitable only if the default Left position continues to be support for the EU; if there is the possibility of accepting or even welcoming a Brexit and turning it to the advantage of Left politics, then the defeat is not inevitable. In the article I asked the question, why is there no British Bernie Sanders? A Brexit might allow one to appear, since it would transform the political landscape in very many ways. Without it, it is hard to see any such revival of the Left at a popular level.

More substantial are the other two groups of responses. One concentrates on the possible economic damage of a Brexit, damage which (it is argued) will necessarily affect the poor more than the rich. This is of course the central argument of the official Remain campaign, but it is a frustrating one in many ways. Much of the debate has simply consisted in citing authorities, and in the process the Left has found itself in the odd position of treating as sages economists and think-tanks it would normally disregard in (say) a general election – how often have socialist policies been criticised by those same authorities? The tone of the economic debate is indeed exactly like that of a general election, in which each side seizes upon suggestions by economists that support their case and disregard the rest. That is understandable when there are reasonable arguments of a non-economic kind to incline people towards their particular party, and when the economic arguments are rhetoric; but in this instance, allegedly, it is *only* the economic considerations upon which people are basing their decision. This is highly dangerous: there are perfectly good economists, particularly in the US where they can take a more neutral view, who argue that Brexit would make little economic difference to the UK. For example, Ashoka Mody, formerly the assistant director of the IMF's European Department and now the Charles and Marie Robertson Professor at Princeton, published a formidable article in *The Independent* on 31 May refuting point by point the claims of the British Treasury, and accusing the community of economists of 'groupthink' on the subject. Mody is easily as well qualified as everyone else in the debate, and has been closer to the economics of the EU than most; we could add to him Mervyn King, the former Governor of the Bank of England, who knows what he is talking about and has described the Remain campaign's economic arguments as 'wildly exaggerated'. Relying on authority, in this area as in most others, is a risky intellectual strategy.

There are in fact a number of features of the economic relationship between the UK and the EU which are rarely mentioned in the debate. For example, as of 2014 the UK ran a balance-of-trade deficit with eighteen of the twenty-seven member countries of the EU, and a surplus of less than £1 billion with each of another eight. But it had a trade surplus of almost £10 billion with the remaining country: Ireland.[8] What this illustrates is that almost all statistics which treat the EU as a single economic unit, from the point of view of the UK, are grossly misleading; strip out Ireland and the EU looks very different. Given the high degree of integration of the Irish and British economies (indeed, I have heard it said that the Irish economy is more integrated into the English economy than the Scottish one is), it is inconceivable that post-Brexit the close economic relationship will not continue, even if there are some minor tariffs; after all, having separate currencies potentially adds more costs to import/export trade than the kinds of tariffs which might be imposed post-Brexit.

And it is not clear whether there would be tariffs of any significance. 'Project Fear' has insinuated that in the event of Brexit the UK would be punished by the imposition of trading barriers, but some calm reflection would show that that is highly implausible. Most of the debate in Britain has concentrated on the self-interest of EU countries in continuing to trade easily with Britain, but that is really the least of it. Under WTO rules to which all the relevant countries have signed up, it is simply illegal to raise tariffs once they have been agreed at a particular level; moreover, punitive tariffs unjustified by domestic economic consid-erations are exactly the things which the WTO came into existence to prevent. And for the second- or third-largest economy in the world (the EU minus Britain) to impose punitive tariffs on the fifth- or sixth-largest (Britain) would be to move decisively into an era of global protectionism and trade warfare with implications going far beyond Europe. Both 'Remainers' and 'Brexiters' are fixated on ways of remaining legally in the single market, but it is not at all clear that in the modern trading world single regional markets matter very much, except (as I said in my article) as devices to enforce a certain kind of neoliberal economic policy.

The third set of objections to my article amount to the claim that I am guilty of baby-boomer utopian nostalgia, and that a realistic view of the modern world, and of current British politics, shows that a revival of classic Labour policies in the UK is simply impossible. On the charge that I am a baby-boomer, I plead guilty (I could scarcely not do so). I would say, however, that there is a romance of realism as well as a romance of utopianism – indeed, realism is often a form of utopianism. The self-image of the realist is as someone who has seen truths which their idealistic contemporaries disregard, and who has thereby gained a special insight into the future; but a genuinely realistic sense of politics shows us that idealists often triumph. More to the point, no one to my knowledge has given a convincing account of why policies and attitudes that were possible in the 1940s and again in the 1960s should not be possible again. My central claim in the article was that we should not overlook the *self-imposed* character of the constraints under which the Left now labours. Just as the US Constitution almost made the New Deal impossible, and it was largely FDR's long term in office which enabled him to create an amenable Supreme Court, so the new constitutional order of the EU makes radical policies in Britain impossible, and no British government can change the character of the European courts. It is easy to come to think of these kinds of structures as facts of nature – exactly that has happened with the US Constitution in the past fifty years, and it is now hard to see any decisive changes in it. But they are *not* facts of nature.

The 'realists' say that the global situation has changed, and that we can no longer have (they often say to me) 'socialism in one country'. But was what the Attlee government put in place 'socialism in one country'? Were the Scandinavian welfare states in their heyday 'socialism in one country'? Is a world of interdependent but independent states, much like the world for most of the modern era, now impossible? If socialism has to wait for a global state, or even a European state, then most people who currently call themselves socialists may as well abandon the label, since there is no foreseeable route to what they want: that is the inevitable consequence of their 'realism'. I have a more limited ambition, but (I would say) in practice a more genuinely realistic one, that the scope for Left politics can be broadened in Britain beyond its current narrow confines. But that is only possible if the political structures in Britain once again permit it.

17 July 2017:
Brexit: A Prize in
Reach for the Left

On 23 June 2016 the referendum on Britain's membership of the European Union was held, and the result was 51.9% Leave and 48.1% Remain. England outside London voted by 242 districts to 52 for Leave, and Wales by 17 districts to 5. London voted 28 districts to 5 for Remain, Northern Ireland 11 districts to 7 for Remain, and all the Scottish districts voted for Remain. Districts were not necessarily Parliamentary constituencies, but it has been calculated that 64% of Labour constituencies and 74% of Conservative constituencies voted Leave.

A year later, on 8 June 2017, the British general election, which Theresa May had called in the hope of increasing her majority, produced a result in which the Conservatives held 317 seats (13 fewer than in the previous Parliament), Labour 232 (30 more), the SNP 35 (21 fewer), and the other parties 29 (9 more). May formed a minority government with support from the DUP. On 17 July I gave a lecture at Policy Exchange entitled 'Brexit: A Prize in Reach for the Left', responding to all these developments.[9] This is the full text of the lecture.

One of my favourite political quotations is the observation by Lord Melbourne on the failure of the Catholic

Emancipation Act to improve the conditions of Irish Catholics: 'What all the wise men promised has not happened, and what all the damned fools said would happen has come to pass.'[10] Well, the damned fools scored an even greater triumph with the Brexit vote. I count myself among them, not in the sense that I predicted the result – like most people in a profession, I assumed that my colleagues (in this case the empiricist political scientists – the wise men of our time) knew what they were doing – but in the sense that I could see the appeal of Brexit to a much greater part of the electorate than seemed to many people to be the case before the referendum. In an article published in the American journal *Dissent* in May last year, and in some follow-up pieces, I argued that the left wing of British politics would benefit significantly from Brexit – actually, though I did not say this then, even more than the Right would do. This was for two reasons.

The first was what you might call a purely tactical consideration, namely the issue of Scottish independence. The Labour Party has virtually never won a general election purely on English votes; England is and almost always has been a fundamentally Tory country. So the prospect of a left-wing party re-establishing itself in England depends on a continuation of the Union, and, I argued, it was the EU which had undermined the British Union by offering the Scots a largely costless path to independence. Almost everything which the Act of Union guaranteed to Scotland as an economy integrated with England was equally guaranteed to it by the European Union. The SNP realised this in the mid-1980s, and its dramatic change of policy on the Common Market (to which before then it had been deeply hostile) was the prelude to its electoral success. But Scottish independence was only costless in this fashion if *both* countries remained in the EU: even if an independent Scotland could remain in the EU after England had left, something the SNP leaders often fantasise about, the costs of disunion for the Scots would escalate dramatically, both economically and psychically. So Brexit, I claimed, was likely to stall the movement towards independence in Scotland.

The second reason that I thought Brexit would help the Left was more fundamental. It was that the essential character of the EU, as Wolfgang Streeck has powerfully argued, is hostile to traditional socialism of the mid-twentieth-century variety. (It is, incidentally, testimony to the remarkably impoverished nature of the British debate on the EU that it has failed to generate any analysis of comparable seriousness and sophistication to that found on the Continent, particularly – I would say – in the writings of Streeck, Habermas and Varoufakis, except perhaps in the work of Chris Bickerton at Cambridge.[11]) If Britain left the EU, I argued, the space available to left-wing policies would suddenly expand, and all sorts of possibilities, including such things as thoroughgoing nationalisation or differential regional taxes, would be on the table again. I will return to this issue in much more detail presently.

So I reasoned; but I did not expect that I would see these effects so quickly! I think the presumption that Brexit would now take place played a major part in the recent general election. In Scotland it must surely have helped to turn the tide against the SNP, making a significant number of people recoil from the idea of a Scotland detached from England under the new circumstances. This is, incidentally, entirely compatible with the way Scots voted in the Brexit referendum – there was every reason for Scots who sympathised with independence to vote Remain in a UK-wide poll, but that is very different from voting for an independent Scotland to stay in the EU separately from England, though the SNP leadership, naturally enough, have conflated the two things. And in England, Jeremy Corbyn felt able to put forward a manifesto which not only endorsed leaving the EU (more clearly than some people are now claiming, since it promised an end to the free movement of labour, something incompatible with the single market, and the creation of new trade agreements with the rest of the world, which is incompatible with the customs union), but also included policies which would have seemed mainstream for the Labour Party during the thirty years after the War, the *trente glorieuses* as Thomas Piketty has labelled those three decades in post-war history, but which would at the very least be hard to implement within the EU as currently configured. And it was these policies, or at least the attitude which underpinned them, which – it is generally agreed – produced a new kind of enthusiasm for the Labour Party.

A corollary of this was the complete implosion of UKIP. In the months after the US election of November 2016, I often found myself arguing against people in America who thought that Trump and Brexit were the same phenomenon. On my view, Brexit was in fact an inoculation *against* Trump and the politics of the radical Right. Leaving the EU would not only kill Scottish independence, it would also the kill the kind of right-wing politics in England which UKIP represented, since it was largely driven by a sense of powerlessness. The feeling – and it need be no more than that – that the political process could after all be responsive to what people wanted even on fundamental matters would immediately remove the emotional force from the radical Right's message, and that too duly seems to have happened. Compare UKIP's performance in the 2017 general election with Trump's, or with Marine Le Pen's, or the radical Right's performance in almost any Western country today. As in the 1930s, Britain may have dodged the bullet of a kind of fascism, and largely because its political structures once again *permit* rather than *constrain* radical politics. This is a lesson which needs to be learned more widely: the more one attempts to use constitutional or cultural power (these being largely the same thing) to suppress dangerous and distasteful political movements, the stronger they grow, for the members of the movements now possess a justifiable case against their rulers.

Related to this is what I think is a widespread misunderstanding about the role immigration from the EU played. The general right of EU citizens to come to Britain is a very clear example of powerlessness on the part of the British authorities. There are many other examples, as we shall see, which to a liberal on immigration like myself are more important, but it is perhaps the most visible and concrete case, and we have carefully and responsibly to distinguish between a general hostility to immigrants and the desire to have an immigration policy. It is, I believe, quite strictly parallel to the hostility to illegal immigration in the US; it is (at least to my mind) anxiety about its *illegality*, and the fact that certain kinds of liberals do not seem to care about this, which angers many people, since it too is an example of the ordinary political processes ceasing to have any effect. I do not see in the US any desire, for example, to repeal the 1965 Immigration Act, which removed racial quotas from the US immigration system, which one might expect if there was a revival there of pre-1965 racism in immigration; and one should not forget that the same voters who voted for Trump had, in many cases, voted for a black President four years earlier. In this respect I think that Jeremy Corbyn and Boris Johnson, who both want a generous immigration policy after Brexit, may have a better instinct about British public opinion than the people who simply accuse the British voters of racism – though one can see why that accusation is a very useful one to make for opponents of Leave.

However, the weeks after the general election have seen signs of a retreat from the clarity offered by the Brexit vote. Remainers, particularly of a familiar world-weary sort, say that this is because the clarity was an illusion, and the full implications of Brexit are only now dawning; but to think this is essentially to make the same mistake which British politicians, and to some degree the whole of British society, have always made about the character of the EU. It is to confuse what one might call *policy* with *constitutional principle*. The vote in the referendum was a vote on a constitutional issue, and questions of policy have now to be decided within this new framework – though the framework allows a very wide range of options. Indeed, the striking and unusual fact about the vote is that it was a vote to put in place a *less* restrictive constitutional framework than has been the case since 1973.

The British have always shied away from considerations of constitutional structures, apart from a familiar type of crank with over-detailed schemes for electoral reform, etc.; but the EU *has* to be thought about in these terms. To adapt Trotsky's thought on the dialectic, you may not be interested in constitutions, but constitutions are interested in you. This is something which it is easier for Britons to see if they think about the US. They are used to understanding American politics against the background of the Constitution, partly because Americans famously keep emphasising that themselves, with oaths of loyalty to the Constitution and so on, and they are familiar with the idea that a critical issue in a Presidential election is the ability to determine political outcomes for a generation via the appointment of justices to the Supreme Court. But close to 700 years of a very different kind of political system (I say 700 years, since the essential principles of Parliamentary legislation and taxation were largely the creation of Edward III in order to fight the Hundred Years' War with public support) have left the British with very different instincts about their own politics.

So deeply imbued have we been with the idea that Parliament, and therefore general elections, can in principle change any features of our common life, that the argument about the EU has almost entirely been an argument about what kind of policies we want to pursue at the moment. The most striking feature of the referendum debate itself was that it was to a great extent conducted as if it was a normal British general election, in which matters of policy were to be decided for the next five years or so. The argument about levels of immigration which came to dominate the debate, at least in some quarters, exemplified this: it was largely concerned with the desirability or otherwise of specific numbers or types of immigrants, as if what was at stake was the British government's immigration policy over the next few years. I was even told explicitly by a number of anti-Brexit friends that what mattered was preventing a Tory victory in the referendum, and that the issues in debate could be sorted out later. This approach was reassuring, in a way, since it showed that at an instinctive level the British still thought of politics as something which was open to change at the ballot box; but in this particular setting the old instincts proved to be an impediment to clear thinking about the issues.

For some years before the referendum I had been trying to get clear in my own mind how to theorise the US Constitution, and I came to think that Britain's relationship with the EU made sense, rather surprisingly, in the same terms. I tried to explain the approach in lectures delivered at Cambridge in 2012, which subsequently appeared as my *The Sleeping Sovereign* in 2016; I didn't discuss the EU directly in the lectures, but it was already at the back of my mind, and my *Dissent* piece drew on the thoughts I had had four years earlier. Briefly, what I argued was that we should take seriously the distinction which some major seventeenth- and eighteenth-century political theorists drew between *sovereignty* and *government*. For hundreds of years it had been assumed that democracy of the ancient kind was impossible in a modern state, since the population could not meet to deliberate in a nation the size of France or England. All that might be possible was a system of representation (hailed as the great modern – i.e. medieval – invention by eighteenth-century historians), but that was not democracy in the ancient or the natural sense of the term, in which the people *legislate*; Aristotle, for example, had described election as an aristocratic principle, since it picked out a limited set of legislators.

What eighteenth-century theorists realised, above all Rousseau, but many of the American founders as well, was that popular legislation on *fundamental* matters was not impeded by the size or character of a modern state. *Government*, to use their term, had to be conducted by small groups or even a single person, able to deliberate and devote all their time to the issues; but *sovereignty* could be expressed in the occasional creation or amendment of fundamental laws which would form a constitution. The referendum naturally followed as a means of occasional popular legislation on constitutional matters, the very first in the world being in Massachusetts in 1778 when the new constitution of the independent state was put to the vote of all the citizens. Other American states followed suit, and even the Federal Constitution, though not put to a referendum, was designed to be ratified in a series of popular assemblies. Revolutionary France then embarked on the most extensive experiment with constitutional referendums, and though they fell into abeyance after the Revolution, interest in constitutional referendums revived in the late nineteenth century and again after the Second World War, until they became the norm in almost all European countries and in all but one of the states of the USA.

Once the distinction between acts of sovereignty and acts of government was in place it was possible to assign the role of constitutional legislator to non-democratic institutions as well – indeed, the two earliest theorists of the distinction, Hobbes and Bodin, assigned it to monarchs. But the distinction was always more relevant to democracy than to any other system of fundamental legislation, for the obvious reason that a monarch or an aristocratic board was not impeded in exercising acts of government as well as acts of sovereignty, and both Bodin and Hobbes seem, surprisingly, to have understood this.

Britain historically had kept out of this story, retaining its medieval representative institution and treating what elsewhere would be constitutional laws, passed in a special way, as merely ordinary statutes. But accession to the EU changed this. (Incidentally, it is often said that Britain has an unwritten constitution and the US a written one. This is not really true: there are many constitutional conventions in the US, as there would have to be, and there are written laws which are patently constitutional in the UK, such as the Act of Settlement, the Act of Union, and the 1972 European Communities Act. The difference is not whether the rules are written or unwritten, but who does the writing, and whether they are a different and more democratic body than the one which writes the ordinary legislation of the country.)

The right way to theorise the EU, I argue, is as in effect a coordinated set of constitutional structures for each of the member countries. The EU is not a 'superstate', nor can it easily become one, juridically: it has always been clearly stated by the highest legal authorities in each country that, at least at the moment, the member countries are sovereign entities, able in the last resort to decide their own futures. This is not empty rhetoric since, among other things, it is the justification for the continued representation of each EU country separately at the UN, something they are extremely unlikely ever to renounce. For this reason much of the use of the term 'sovereignty' in the referendum debate was indeed as unhelpful as its critics complained. Moreover, the fact that the EU is not a state is the source of many of the problems it itself faces, as well as the problems conventional states face dealing with it; the thousands of deaths in the Mediterranean are testimony to the dangers of its current anomalous character and the fact that it is stuck in a half-way house, able to be neither a state with its own borders nor an alliance of states which control their own. It is also why negotiating with it is not like negotiating with a normal state, but more in some ways (though one should not push this analogy too far) like negotiating with a Supreme Court – the picture Varoufakis paints in his gripping memoirs of his dealings with the EU institutions illustrates their strange character and the mistake we make if we treat it like either a unitary state or an ordinary international grouping.

The key feature of the EU is that the sovereign authority in each state has enacted a certain rather curious kind of constitutional order for each of them, in which a set of principles and institutions are entrenched in a position beyond the reach of conventional, 'governmental', legislation. These principles and institutions are supranational in character, of course, and that is why the states took this course of action. But seen from within each state the supranational character is not, in a way, the key feature: the key feature is rather that they are entrenched within the legal system of each country (this is what makes them different from the other supranational arrangements with which they are often compared, such as NATO or – even – the UN, at least in great part). The curious feature of these constitutional orders, however, is that they cannot be *amended* by the same process by which they were imposed: an Act of the UK Parliament by itself straightforwardly entrenched the EU institutions in UK law, but no Act of the UK Parliament by itself can amend them. Only a process of intergovernmental negotiation, issuing in changes which no one country can impose upon itself, can alter the essential character of the EU's constitutional structure. The only thing an individual state can do is repudiate the *whole* structure – as we are finding out.

Most states on the Continent already had constitutional structures of some sort before the EU was formed, and their politicians were used to operating inside them, just as American politicians are. But the idea that a constitution could not be amended was new to them also – though, and this may be significant, not to *German* politicians. The German Constitution is a legal oddity: the West German Constitution, the *Grundgesetz*, was technically authorised by three of the four powers in the Allied military government, and included the provision that in the event of reunification a new constitution would have to be ratified by the German people. After the dissolution of the military government in 1991, the provinces of East Germany simply acceded to the western state and its *Grundgesetz*, so the German Constitution has never actually been ratified properly. Moreover, a tradition has developed within German constitutional jurisprudence of supposing that certain fundamental moral principles are enshrined in constitutional law without the need for positive enactment. It is easy to see how a domestic structure of this kind renders the structures of the EU far less problematic for Germany than they are for the UK, or indeed for France, with its long history of popular constitutional legislation.

Britain, by virtue of its desire to join what was then the Common Market, thus found itself forced unwittingly into the default shape of a modern state, with a constitution which lay beyond the power of the *government* to change. And as an almost instinctive recognition of this, the Wilson administration as we all know decided to use for the first time the default institution of constitutional legislation in a modern state, the referendum, in order to legitimate it. Though constitutional referendums had occasionally been proposed in the UK, notably to deal with Irish (and indeed Scottish) Home Rule, this was the first time that such a thing had seemed clearly necessary in Britain – about 200 years after it seemed equally clearly necessary to the English settlers in Massachusetts. Since that time, as we also all know, constitutional referendums have become a familiar feature of British political life. Characteristically, this has happened without a formal or legal acknowledgment of their fundamental role, and technically they are merely consultative; but the idea that they could be disregarded seems to most people about as fanciful as the idea that the Queen could actually use the power, still technically in her hands, to veto a Parliamentary statute. Even in the aftermath of the Brexit vote, few people have advocated simply ignoring the result; the popular anti-Brexit response has been instead to call for a second vote, and that seems to me to be testimony to the obviousness of the change that has come over British politics. The EU and the referendum as an institution in the UK are wrapped in one another's arms.

I might add at this point that the dangers and disadvantages of these kinds of structures tend to be far less obvious to people who are politically engaged or have some kind of public role. I mix in America with people who are regularly dealing with the Supreme Court, are leading figures in the political parties, or are writing for the press and trying to influence the political agenda. For them, it is easier to think that they will have some effect on politics through these processes than through the old-fashioned process of elections, and it is natural for them to think that their personal experience is something like an objective fact. One of the critical comments on my Brexit piece concluded with something like 'perhaps we have had too much democracy'; it struck me reading it that 'we' would not have to worry about less democracy if 'we' were people like you and me, but for most people the vote is the one way they possess of altering their political circumstances. As a result, I think the general population has always been able to think more clearly about the EU than the political elites, since they have much more to lose.

To repeat: you may not be interested in constitutions, but constitutions are interested in you. They are not neutral, benign forces, however much the lawyers charged with maintaining them pretend that this is so; again, you only have to think about the history of American constitutional jurisprudence (much more familiar to us than Continental constitutional jurisprudence, for obvious reasons) to see this. Think about the way the Commerce Clause has been used to extend federal power; think about the Dred Scott judgment and its endorsement of slavery; think about the Korematsu case on the internment of Japanese Americans; think about Citizens United. Put against them, of course, *Brown v. the Board of Education* or *Roe v. Wade*; but we will be choosing according to our political preferences. Certain kinds of political programmes are simply impossible in certain kinds of constitutional orders.

My favourite example of this, and something of great relevance to the general theme of this lecture, is the creation of the National Health Service in Britain. It required a very unusual constitutional order, since its most distinctive feature, and the thing which still sharply differentiates it from the single-payer systems found in most developed countries (and even, in many respects, in the US), was the fact that it involved a mass expropriation of private property, in the form of the so-called 'voluntary' hospitals, some of which like Barts had been independent institutions for over 800 years. This was the issue which was most fiercely debated within the Attlee Cabinet, and the result of Nye Bevan's victory there was one of the most far-reaching examples of nationalisation from those years, and the only one which has survived more or less intact. It is often asked by opponents of the NHS, 'if it's so good, why don't other countries copy it?' But in this respect it would be extremely difficult for other countries to copy it, since in most modern states expropriation of private property without compensation would be legally impossible without a far-reaching constitutional amendment which might be very hard to pass. In Britain in 1946 all that was needed was a single sentence in an Act of Parliament: 'there shall, on the appointed day, be transferred to and vest in the Minister by virtue of this Act all interests in or attaching to premises forming part of a voluntary hospital or used for the purposes of a voluntary hospital ...' (para. 6.1). What this illustrates is that the achievements of the Attlee government, still the touchstone for left-wing measures in this country, required the kind of ancient omnicompetence which Parliament still possessed in the 1940s.

The fact that the British labour movement was intensely Parliamentary and non-revolutionary (as every schoolchild is taught – or are they still?) was not the consequence of some magical trait of the British which enabled them to avoid the turmoils of the revolutionary years on the Continent (and indeed in America, for what else was the Civil War but a vast revolutionary moment?). Marx and Engels observed from their vantage point in Victorian England that the bourgeoisie had taken different routes in France and England to hamper the industrial working class from gaining power. In France they had conceded universal male suffrage, first in 1792 and again and permanently in 1848, but they had bound the legislature with a constitution which secured things such as private property (broadly defined) against legislative encroachment. In England, there were no such constraints on the legislature, and therefore the proletariat had to be denied the vote – which in this country, we should remember, was finally extended to the entire adult male population only in 1918, the same year that the first women received it (or rather recovered it – women lost the vote in 1832). So Marx and Engels concluded that the only thing necessary to bring about socialism in England was the extension of the Parliamentary franchise, whereas in France it required revolutionary and extra-constitutional action. Exactly the same logic activated the early leaders of the Labour Party in Britain: they had every confidence that the Parliamentary route to power was the right one, since they would then have available to them any measures to promote socialism which they thought fit, and which they could persuade a simple majority of their country (by definition, largely the working class) to support.

In the case of the EU, the overall character of the constitutional order pushes consistently in what we might call a neoliberal direction. This is the point which Wolfgang Streeck has repeatedly insisted on, and has documented in convincing detail; he thinks that it is largely because of the influence of German capital on the EU institutions, and that is clearly true to an extent, but I would also argue that the institutions to some degree have a life of their own. Put in place a constitutional order which specifies certain economic freedoms (for the EU, the now notorious four freedoms, the free movement of goods, capital, services and labour, to which we should also add the lesser-known but very important freedom of establishment, i.e. the right to set up a new business in any country of the union), let a group of modern jurists loose on them, and the result will almost inevitably be a series of rules which are tilted towards the market. Constitutional orders are a combination of rules and the people interpreting them (as Hobbes in particular understood very well), and the people inevitably develop a certain kind of internal culture which is usually proudly immune to outside political pressures. The American founders realised this, and were very interested in ways in which the judicial process could be made responsive to the citizens, including in some states in the election of judges, and in the elaborate process of nomination and confirmation for federal judges. The worst of all worlds is to have a strong constitutional order and an independent judiciary – something I sometimes fear Britain is drifting towards even outside the EU. But that would be material for another day.

A simple way of seeing how this works is through a comparison of Bernie Sanders and Jeremy Corbyn. As many people have observed, the parallels between them are very close, in terms of their age, their lack of conventional politicians' gloss, their roles as insurgents within an established centre-left party, and the enthusiastic support they receive from young voters. The three proposals which Sanders put at the heart of his movement were: pull out of or radically modify NAFTA and do not enter the TPP; greatly increase the tax on the big Wall Street banks; and introduce free state college and university tuition paid for largely by the Wall Street tax. The British version of these proposals obviously resonate with Labour's newly energised electorate, but – and I want to stress this – *none of them would have been feasible for a British government within the EU.*

The EU was itself Britain's NAFTA or TPP, and it also decided all questions of trade for Britain with the rest of the world, so there would be no question of a British Bernie within the EU even thinking of such a thing. A British government could theoretically change the tax regime for the City, but the free movement of labour and capital within the EU would permit the banks simply to transfer operation to a friendlier tax regime elsewhere in the European Union without anything of the trauma which would afflict Wall Street banks if they fled the US to avoid a Bernie tax. And even something (one would have thought) as parochial as free college tuition would not have been entered into lightly by a Britain within the EU. The EU enforces the principle that no distinction can be made between home and EU students when it comes to college fees, so free tuition funded by British taxes for British students (assuming that the banks could be made to stand still long enough to be taxed) would mean free tuition for students from across the EU funded by the British. Scotland has managed this on a small scale, though with the significant anomaly that it can charge fees to English students but not to other EU ones, but it is inconceivable that a scheme of this kind could be put in place for the whole of Britain without enormous public protest. I should say that I am amazed that the tabloids didn't leap long ago onto the fact that British taxpayers already subsidise EU students in English universities, far more in practice than other EU taxpayers subsidise British students at Continental universities. Strikingly, the EU enforces a rule which would be unacceptable even in the integrated economy of the US, since it is taken for granted there that in-state students pay lower fees at state univer-sities than out-of-state students.

If what I have been saying so far is right, the worst mistake which the Left in Britain could make would be to once again put itself under these kinds of constraint. Paradoxically, the constraints do not affect the Right anything like as much; indeed, I would say that the under-lying verities of the EU are currently just the same as they were in the 1970s, when Margaret Thatcher wore her famous Common Market jumper, and a wide swathe of Labour politicians, from Michael Foot through Tony Benn (who in those days was not thought to be exceptionally left-wing) to Peter Shore, who was generally on the right of the party, all saw the risks to traditional Labour politics which European union posed. This is why Corbyn, a relic (like myself) from the 1970s, could see this more clearly than other contemporary politicians. This particular penny is beginning to drop on the Right – I was very struck by a recent piece in *The Telegraph* by Charles Moore, raising the question of whether it might be best to stay within the institutions of the EU in order to block Corbyn's policies. To his credit, he answered his question decisively in the negative, but his article reminds us about the odd history of European union, and how its critical aspect has always been the role of union in removing possibilities from domestic politics, though political parties have seldom been able to admit this, even to themselves.[12] The Tories were enthusiastic about it as a means of permanently blocking the reappearance of socialism, but turned against it when under Delors it looked as if it would instead entrench left-wing policies; Labour became interested in it at that point, though some (but rather few) Labour politicians began to turn against it more recently when it turned out that the actual decisions of the European institutions by and large go against the interests of European workers. It should also be said that there has always been a significant section of the Labour Party which viewed EU membership as a kind of self-denying ordinance, preventing the party from veering back to the Left and therefore (they thought) endangering its electoral prospects – this is, I think, the honourable (though I would say misguided) source of the strange fascination it has held for some important figures in the party. But the key point about this history is that it is precisely the capacity of European union to take serious political issues off the domestic agenda that has been the fundamental reason *both* for supporting it *and* for opposing it.

So what should the Left now do? There has been a remarkable outbreak in the press and at Westminster of people trying to engineer a 'soft' Brexit. Astonishingly, the idea seems to have gained ground in some quarters that the Labour vote in the general election was a vote against Brexit; this is an idea that could only occur to people in the Left establishment who believe that in reality most Labour Party voters must be just like them, and for some reason were merely pretending to be in favour of Brexit last year. This is testimony to the extraordinary power of the conviction among most politically active people that to be on the Left simply entails support for the EU, and that sooner or later everyone will realise this; it is also testimony to the social gulf between the Left establishment and its traditional electorate.

In particular, something like membership of the EEA is creeping back onto the agenda. At the beginning of the referendum campaign, like many Brexiteers at that time, I was mildly in favour of the EEA option, but I have come to realise its dangers. First, from the point of view of keeping Scotland in the Union it is not really an improvement on the EU. Scotland would still not need the United Kingdom to have a united economy with England, and the logic of that position would sooner or later work itself out; Norway after all manages to have an integrated economy with the rest of Scandinavia without being under Danish rule. This is presumably why Nicola Sturgeon seems reasonably happy with a soft Brexit. Ruth Davidson is also supposedly pushing for it; this could simply be a piece of local political tactics, but she might mean it, and if so she may not so easily be able to see off the next push for independence. Indeed, she might easily find herself in a few years' time Prime Minister of an independent Scotland, and who knows whether this has occurred to her or not?

Second, the arguments about the restrictions on Left policies which the EU institutions represent apply just as much to the EEA or EFTA. By now the laws in EEA and EFTA countries on such things as competition are thoroughly integrated into the EU legal framework, and are governed by ECJ judgments. As long as this is so, the EEA and EFTA will have broadly the same economic character as the EU. This has already been seen in Norway, where a collective agreement dating from the 1970s which granted the Norwegian dock labourers' union the sole right to unload cargo was nullified by the Norwegian Supreme Court earlier this year on the grounds of its incompatibility with EU law by virtue of the freedom of establishment clause; this parallels a similar case within the EU, currently going through the courts in Spain. Breaking the comparable arrangement with dock workers which the Labour government negotiated in 1947, we should remember, was one of Thatcher's signal achievements. And though some defenders of this 'soft' Brexit talk about it as a temporary measure, if there is one safe generalisation in politics, it is that temporary arrangements usually become permanent.

If I am right in supposing that this new surge in left-wing politics is the result of Brexit, it would be suicidal to overturn it. We can see the dangers of doing so very clearly in the case of the working-class UKIP voters, particularly in the North, who felt it was now safe to return to Labour; but it is also dangerous indirectly and in the long term for the newly energised younger voters of the South. They may to some degree support the EU, but their new energy is a product of Brexit, and not in the sense that it is merely a *reaction* to it. Like everyone else, they have sensed the opening up of possibilities long denied to them, and even if they want the EU they surely do not want the return to power of the kind of politician the EU necessarily breeds. I suppose the closest analogue to the position we can reasonably ascribe to them is not Streeck's but Varoufakis's: a hope that somehow the EU can be seized by the forces of the Left, coming especially from Southern Europe. As I said earlier, the views of both Streeck and Varoufakis are way beyond anything available in the British debate about Europe in their seriousness and sophistication, but the problem with Varoufakis's position is that he has never given any good reasons for supposing his vision is attainable; the more sober view espoused by Streeck carries more conviction, and its lesson (as he has himself acknowledged) is that Brexit may be the best hope, not only for Britain but for the rest of Europe as a whole. The great prize awaiting the Left in Britain, and it is now almost within reach, is genuine Brexit followed by a Labour government. Then the Left can re-enact whatever it thinks is good in EU regulations about such things as the environment and working conditions, and whatever immigration policy it wishes, and at the same time free itself from the far-reaching restrictions which the EU imposes on traditional socialism.

But the Labour Party is faced with a tremendous temptation: undermine the May government by joining with those in the Conservative Party who want a soft Brexit, and profit from the Conservatives' consequent dissolution. But if the Labour Party chooses short-term success by re-entering (in some form) these structures, the logic of British politics over the last thirty years will simply repeat itself, and we will inevitably end up with permanent Tory rule in an England without Scotland, or some kind of Blairite regime, no doubt repackaged (barely) as 'Macronist' – Macron being the perfect emblem of the conjunction of the EU and neoliberal economic policies, and the consequent destruction of socialism. Without Brexit the Labour Party will revert to its role of providing an alternative managerial class for late-stage capitalism, and the enthusiasm of its new-found supporters will wither away or find new and more troubling outlets. This is exactly what the Tory Remainers would like to see happen, and the Labour leadership ought not to fall into their trap. But the signs are not good, with Keir Starmer insisting that some deal must be struck with the EU and that a 'hard' Brexit will necessarily be opposed in Parliament by the Labour Party. Above all, the Labour Party needs to keep its nerve: it is on the verge of its greatest prize in a couple of generations, with the possibility of genuinely transforming British politics, and it would be a tragedy if it allowed itself to throw this away.

16 August 2017

On 23 June 2017 negotiations formally opened between the UK and the EU over a Withdrawal Agreement, and on 13 July the government introduced the European Union (Withdrawal) Bill, which eventually received the royal assent on 26 June 2018. On 15 August the government published a paper on customs arrangements with the EU, proposing 'a model of close association with the EU Customs Union for a time-limited interim period'.

The central fact about the British relationship with the EU is that by the end of the twentieth century the Labour and Conservative parties had changed places on the issue. In the debates of the 1960s and 1970s about joining or staying in the EEC, many leading figures in the Labour Party expressed great suspicion about what membership would mean for the future of socialism in the UK, but only a few Conservatives expressed any opposition to it. The young Margaret Thatcher, famously, was photographed wearing a jumper featuring all the flags of the Common Market. By 2000 exactly the opposite was true, as large numbers of Tory backbenchers and some ministers had turned against the EU, at the same time as hostility to it could barely be voiced within the mainstream of the Labour Party. The remarkable thing about this, however, is that the underlying logic of the situation remained the same: on any reasonable analysis of the EU, both its structure and its policies were largely inimical to the traditional Left, and largely friendly to late twentieth-century capitalism.

When Macmillan's government first applied for membership of the EEC, the dominant strain in the Labour Party was opposed to it, with a major concern of the left of the party being that membership would limit the possibility of a planned economy. This was still entirely obvious in the great discussion inside Wilson's Cabinet at Chequers on 22 October 1966 which effectively committed the Labour Party, and therefore in effect British governments of whatever political complexion, to continue to seek entry to the EEC. This was in fact the decisive moment in the history of Britain's relationship with the EU, since it made the cause of Europe for the first time a bi-partisan issue, and therefore one bound in the end to succeed. Richard Crossman, the most acute observer of the events (and the last genuine intellectual to serve in a British Cabinet), recorded in his diary that there had been two key issues: the first was whether the pound would have to be devalued on entry, but the second was 'whether the Commission in Brussels would really deprive us not only of some of our sovereignty but of some of our power to plan the economy? Would investment grants be allowable or not? Would we still be able to see that new factories are put in Scotland rather than in South-East England?'[13] This was the heart of the matter for the socialists in Wilson's government, and a few months later Crossman noted:

Today Barbara [Castle] made a tremendous speech saying that entry would transform our socialism and make us abandon our plans. In a sense she's completely right. If anybody wanted, apart from myself, Britain to be a socialist offshore island, entry to the Market would mean the abandonment of that ideal. Up to the July freeze [on wages, for the last six months of 1966] it was still possible

to believe that we in the Wilson Government would strip
ourselves of the sterling area, withdraw from East of Suez,
and take the Swedish line of socialism ... but now it is felt
by almost everyone that it's too late.[14]

'East of Suez' played to modern eyes a surprising role
in the debates: many even in Wilson's Cabinet thought
that Britain could only sustain its post-imperial role in
the Middle and Far East from within the EEC. As Con
O'Neill, at the time Britain's ambassador to the EEC,
had put it in a staggering memorandum two years earlier:
without membership 'we can decline again to what was
for so long our proper place: but if we choose this course
I feel we must be prepared for the decline to be rather
rapid. In particular, I feel that unless we succeed in
creating a satisfactory relationship with Europe we may
have declined in a relatively short time into neutrality
... a greater Sweden.'[15] Given that by the end of the
century Britain had officially withdrawn its troops from
'East of Suez', had abolished the sterling area, and had
devalued the pound, it would seem that – as so often – the
advice from the Foreign Office had been wrong in every
particular. Who on the Left now, looking back, would not
have preferred Britain to have been a 'greater Sweden' for
all those years, rather than enmeshed in the expensive and
futile task of 'punching above its weight' (something most
skilled boxers advise against)?

Again and again in the discussions which prepared the
British state for entry into the EEC it was post-imperial
politics which preoccupied the participants. It was, for
example, taken for granted that the Americans were
anxious for Britain to join the EEC as part of their own
European schemes. Does anyone on the Left now feel
comfortable about this? And even if by any chance they
are still old-style Labour Cold Warriors, they should
understand that in the end the State Department was
as mistaken as the Foreign Office: once majority voting
came into the EU Britain could no longer single-handedly

advance America's interests within the union, and the grand schemes of the 1960s ultimately came to nothing. Brexiteers have often been accused of nostalgia for Britain's vanished greatness, but as the story of Britain's entry into the EEC shows in abundance, it was the pro-Europeans who were transfixed by a fantasy that Britain could avoid being (in O'Neill's revealing words) in 'our proper place', and the anti-Europeans who were – and still are – the true realists.

The key fact, however, for our present discussions is that the socialists in Wilson's Cabinet were exactly correct even in 1966/7, and the development of the EU since then has fully confirmed their judgment. They were aware that the Treaty of Rome which brought the Common Market into being had enshrined the famous 'four freedoms', the freedom of movement for goods, services, capital and workers, and had created the European Court of Justice to oversee them. The structures of the EEC in the 1960s and 1970s were relatively undeveloped, but it was already obvious that enforcing the four freedoms would cause problems for traditional socialist measures such as nationalisation; it was in 1964 that an Italian case involving the nationalisation of the electricity industry led to the ruling by the ECJ that on such matters the Treaty of Rome took priority over domestic legislation. Nationalisation without compensation was not expressly forbidden, but a series of judgments from the 1970s onwards established the principle that it would normally be impossible, and it was already clear in 1966/7 that that was likely to be the case. Many members of the Wilson government had served in Attlee's administrations (though only Wilson himself had been in Attlee's Cabinet), and they were well aware that the nationalisation measures pushed through in the Attlee years, including above all the creation of the NHS through the nationalisation without compensation of the existing hospitals, would not have been possible within the EEC.

Crossman's anxiety about regional planning was also prescient: the EU has consistently tried to forbid such things as different levels of corporation tax intended to benefit certain regions of member states. Indeed, an often overlooked feature of the push for Scottish independence is that under the EU rules Scotland could not be singled out for special treatment within the United Kingdom in the way the old Labour Party had envisaged. A few gestures towards workers' rights, in many cases quickly undermined by judgments of the ECJ, cannot alter the fact that, as Wolfgang Streeck in particular has repeatedly stressed, the fundamental constitutional structures of the EU tilt it decisively towards what is now termed 'neoliberal' economic policies. The famous speech by Jacques Delors to the TUC in 1988, which is often thought to have led the Labour Party to believe that the constitutional apparatus of the EU could be used in the cause of socialism, turned out very quickly to be a set of empty promises, as anyone who understood the fundamental nature of the EU would have seen at the time – and as Bryan Gould, defeated in the Labour leadership election of 1992, did see.

It is a familiar lament on the Left across Europe that after Thatcher and Reagan the world shifted markedly to the Right, and that social democratic parties had no choice but to follow suit. This was above all the myth of the Blair years. But already in the Wilson discussions a sense of failure hung over the proceedings, as Crossman noted; the demoralisation of at least the British Left, and its willingness to put itself into a system which precluded further steps towards socialism, preceded Thatcher by more than a decade. But it is important to stress that the demoralisation was largely induced by fear of Britain losing its *international* role. Long before Thatcher the British Left was faced with a choice between what many people (wrongly, as it turned out) supposed would be the continuation of Britain's post-war 'great power' status and what was often stigmatised as a 'Little England' policy. Crossman, again, put his finger on the real issue: 'I regard Little England as the precondition for any successful socialist planning whether inside or outside the Common

Market',[16] and he urged the Cabinet to take it seriously as a basis for life outside the EEC. But he failed to convince his colleagues, and though powerful figures from across the Labour spectrum between 1973 and 1975 tried to force the party to withdraw from the EEC after Britain's entry in 1973, they too lost in the referendum campaign of 1975. Naturally the Left had to follow Thatcher's example in the 1980s and 1990s: they were locked into a system which precluded anything else, and the continued attempt to break out of the system had critically wounded the Labour Party, with the defection of some of its leading figures to form the Social Democratic Party. It was not Thatcher who destroyed the prospects of socialism in Britain, but the Labour Party's own loss of nerve over Europe. Something similar was repeated across the whole of the EU, with the result we can now see, that the old socialist parties have in most cases been destroyed.

But not in Britain. Miraculously, a party which before June of this year almost all pundits were consigning to the norm of European oblivion has not only survived but has come close to taking power again. One explanation of this, based on some opinion polling and a great deal of conjecture, is that the party managed to present itself as in some sense anti-Brexit – despite the fact that it was led by someone who was pretty clearly at least half-hearted about the EU, and the fact that its manifesto took for granted that Britain would leave both the single market and the customs union. There may be some truth in this; but much more striking was the fact that both party workers and Labour's old electorate seemed to be newly energised and unwilling to crouch down into the usual posture of defeat. Whether or not the people concerned were fully conscious of the fact, they were for the first time in almost fifty years in a position where the party they supported could offer a large range of new choices, from rail renationalisation to free tuition at English universities. If – though this now looks less plausible – the Labour Party were to relapse into a commitment to membership, it would not take

long for its policies also to relapse into their old rather
trivial character, and for its new-found energy once again
to dissipate. The relative collapse of the SNP can also
be understood in this light: once it came to be believed
that England, at least, would leave the EU, it would not
be surprising if many Scottish voters baulked at erecting
barriers between Scotland and England; independence if
both countries remained within the EU would be virtually
costless, both economically and psychologically, but that
was far from being the case after 23 June 2016.

The attitude of the Labour electorate and, belatedly,
the Labour Party to the EU thus makes perfect sense. The
British working class has never been particularly keen on
Britain's imperial role, suspecting with good reason that
it benefitted their rulers rather than themselves, and now
that the fantasies about that role have receded it is easy
to see the real character of the EU and the damage it has
done to left-wing causes both in the UK and across the
Continent. The real puzzle is why it was the Conservative
Party which precipitated the referendum, and why it was
the party in which the cause of Brexit has until now been
most firmly lodged. It is this fact which has in practice
given many people on the Left their principal reason to
mistrust Brexit, seeing it as inherently a right-wing enterprise. One would have thought that a combination of
neoliberal economic policies, enforced through a constitutional structure which it is almost impossible to change,
and the vision of a Britain which was still acting as a great
power, would have proved irresistible to most Tories, as
indeed it was in the 1960s and 1970s. We might have
attributed Tory hostility to the EU to the explosion of
immigration from Eastern Europe after 2004, except that
Euroscepticism as a significant force in the Tory Party
long predated this – remember John Major's 'bastards'
outburst in 1993. So what happened? Delors is one
explanation – Thatcher in particular is often seen as
changing her stance on Europe when it looked as if it
might become a vehicle for socialism. But by the time

John Major succeeded her such an outcome was looking increasingly improbable, as Major himself obviously understood, and yet Tory Euroscepticism continued to flourish, and indirectly to legitimate its more demotic version in the shape of UKIP.

One answer, which may be difficult for the Left to accept, is that many Tories worked against what might have been thought to be their own political and economic interest because they had a romantic vision of the nation state. As we know, Marx and Engels argued that among the principal victims of capitalism were the old nations, as the bourgeoisie 'through its exploitation of the world market [has] given a cosmopolitan character to production and consumption in every country'.[17] The Tories who opposed this, at least in the form of the EU, might have been what Marx and Engels termed 'Reactionists', but at least they did not run headlong into the arms of world capitalism, as so many on the Left have unwittingly done.

Terror of appearing xenophobic has led the Left to support structures which in happier days they would have been the first to condemn. How is it that so many people in Britain who still think of themselves as socialists could use as conclusive arguments against their opponents that their policies will weaken London's banking industry, or damage the UK's international competitiveness, as if all we can do is join in the race to the bottom prescribed to us by global capitalism? Do they not remember all the times those arguments were used against them, and how they seemed to be merely the cries of anguish from a threatened class? Once, they could easily reply that competitive markets are selective in their distribution of benefits, and need to be controlled in all kinds of ways by democratic politics. Why did they forget this? How have they allowed themselves to be persuaded that people should not make the conditions of their life through political action, but have them made for them by market forces over which they have no control? In short, how did they take on all the attributes of a conservative governing class, and fail to take advantage of the one opportunity they were given to put their old principles into practice?

To continue with the Marxist, or in this instance Hegelian, terminology, there is a kind of cunning of capitalist reason, in which people who call themselves socialists are in fact without realising it doing capitalism's work for it. Those on the Left who continue to support the EU out of what they vaguely feel is a kind of cosmopolitanism are a tragic example of this. In the same way, the Tory Eurosceptics are governed by the cunning of socialist reason: their attachment to the old nation state is what will permit the reappearance of socialist politics in Britain.

6 November 2017

The press on both sides of the Atlantic is full of stories about a 'crisis of democracy'. And there is indeed one, if by 'crisis' we understand the word's original, medical, meaning: the point in an illness at which the patient either dies or recovers. We cannot make sense of the events of 2016 unless we recognise that democracy has been ill for much of the last fifty years, and that this 'crisis' is indeed the point at which it will recover or finally expire.

Once upon a time – and how long ago it now seems – the citizens of Western states recognised that they needed the help of even the poorest of their fellow citizens in constructing the conditions of their common life. The help ranged from the manufacture of much of what they consumed, on a scale far beyond the localised production of the pre-industrial world, to – at its extreme – the creation of the great citizen armies of the twentieth century, which quite literally in many instances saved the lives of even the richest and most powerful members of those states, and in which the ruling class and the working class to a significant extent fought side by side. The recognition that these citizens had to be given a serious voice in what happened to their countries was not based on some vague humanitarian principle: it was based on a concrete understanding of what mass action on the part of the citizens had achieved and (it was thought) would continue to achieve. It is no coincidence, for example, that the great advances in democratic politics tended to take place after these wars of the citizen armies: in Britain all adult males finally achieved the vote only in 1918, at the same time as the suffrage began to be extended to women. Similarly, after 1945 the practical implications of democratic politics were worked out with the policies of the Attlee government. But the scale of the transformation wrought by the mass armies of industrial workers induced something of the same response, independently of warfare: such a crucial population could not be kept in a form of subjection indefinitely. One can go from old movies of the Ford plant in Dearborn, Michigan to movies of the armies in Europe in the Second World War and see exactly the same collective force, and how it had to be respected.

This sense of gratitude to one's fellow citizens was not felt as plainly in the defeated nations of Europe, for obvious reasons. Indeed, after both World Wars, and especially the First, the response of many in the defeated nations was likely to be suspicion of betrayal or resentment at feebleness rather than gratitude. But in Britain and the US, at least, it sustained during the post-war period a general sense of at least potential collaboration between the ruling class and the working class, manifested in such things as the acceptance of powerful unions and a reasonable balance between the rewards of labour and those of capital (the kind of thing traced in Thomas Piketty's book[18]). The high-water mark of those years was the securing of the vote for the African-Americans of the South, though in retrospect that may also have been the final act. And in the defeated nations after the Second World War, above all Germany itself, the sheer scale of the work involved in rebuilding their shattered societies also brought home for many the necessity of relying on all their fellow citizens if they were to succeed in the rebuilding. This, more than anything else, sustained Piketty's *trente glorieuses*.

The central problem of Western societies now, however, and the septicaemia which has invaded the organs of the democracies, is that the concrete benefits which mass action used to deliver are no longer necessary. The history of the citizen army, again, is revealing. The last mass citizen army which Western societies (other than Israel, a very special and unrepresentative case) will ever have seen was the army which fought the Vietnam War, and far from feeling gratitude to it, the American ruling class was terrified by its near mutinous response to a plainly unjust war – though this was exactly what the old theorists of citizen armies, from Machiavelli onwards, took to be one of their points. Never again will there be an American army of the old type; instead we have a relatively small group of expert soldiers and a set of geeks playing deadly video games in a bunker in Iowa. A kind of windy rhetoric in US public discourse about the military mimics the genuine feelings people once had, but it cannot disguise for very long the transformation in what the military represents.

The same is true of industrial power. People in America and Britain now owe very little concretely to one another's efforts: to a far greater extent than sixty years ago, what they consume either comes from overseas or, if made in their own countries, is made with minuscule workforces, and even then often by an immigrant population without the vote. One hundred thousand workers in their pre-war heyday manned the old Ford lines at Dearborn, now there are 6,000. As robots take over yet more production, the numbers of people in productive employment are clearly going to fall even more.

The result of all this has been the creation of what Guy Standing has termed the 'precariat', or what the pseudonymous blogger 'Anne Amnesia' has more vividly and accurately termed the 'unnecessariat'. And one striking consequence of this shift has been a subtle change in political rhetoric. Many politicians on the Left now routinely describe themselves as having gone into politics to *help* their fellow citizens; thus Hillary Clinton said during the Presidential election campaign that she was in the race 'to make life better for children and families' (this was the same speech in which she said, equally revealingly, 'when it comes to public service, I'm better at the service part than the public part'). Listening to this kind of politician one often feels that they think of the state as something like the armed wing of Oxfam. But charity is not a strong enough principle to sustain genuine democracy; apart from anything else, as a long tradition from the ancient world to the eighteenth century recognised, the recipients of charity can come to hate their benefactors, since the acts of benevolence merely reveal ever more clearly the power differential between the people concerned. Moreover, as upward social mobility came to an end during the same period, particularly for the white working class, the cultural gap between the rulers of Western democracies and their electorates grew even wider.

The disappearance of this visceral sense of a collective enterprise permitted the development of institutions which have been described as 'post-democratic', such things as independent central banks, more powerful supreme or constitutional courts, and the intrusion of the market into what used to be publicly managed activities. This fits with the extraordinary discovery by my Harvard colleague Yascha Mounk and his collaborator Roberto Stefan Foa that in all the long-standing Western democracies there is a very precise correlation between the age of respondents in opinion polls and the degree of their commitment to democracy. About 75 per cent of those born in the 1930s believe that it is 'essential' to live in a democracy, but this falls steadily to little more than 25 per cent of those born in the 1980s. And lest this be thought to be a relatively trivial question, the same is true of the answer which people give to the question of whether a military takeover would be legitimate: again, the older respondents are strongly opposed, and the younger ones far less so! Among other things, this finding should give pause to some of the post-Brexit commentary: it may well be true that the older and less educated voters were more supportive of Brexit, but (as other people have observed) 'less educated' is the *same* as 'older', given the staggering expansion of higher education since the 1990s. The fact that older voters are in general both keener on democracy and keener on Brexit is unlikely to be a coincidence.

The response of another political scientist to Mounk and Foa's findings was to say that democratic values are still flourishing, as 'tolerance of minorities' has been steadily increasing over the same period. But this goes to the heart of the matter. It is often casually assumed that tolerance of minorities is part of democratic politics, but it can also often be part of non-democratic politics, as the history of 'enlightened despotism' in eighteenth-century Europe illustrates (a period in European history, incidentally, with marked resemblances to our own – a society of relatively liberal values and the rule of law, but no democratic control). Indeed, despotism of this kind is often defended precisely on the grounds that it does a better job of protecting minorities than full democratic government will do – the fear of the 'tyranny of the majority'. But this has almost always proved to be a highly short-sighted policy. Populations denied democratic expression turn against the minorities whom they see to be the beneficiaries of the unrepresentative political structures with far greater vindictiveness than they would feel if democratic politics were working effectively. The great example of how this can be averted used to be Britain, which had both a reasonably liberal society and a sovereign Parliament completely untrammelled in what it could do by any constitutional constraints, two things which opponents of democratic government think should not go together. Unfortunately, once the fear of the majority is embedded in political institutions it is extremely difficult to reverse course except at great social cost.

17 February 2018

In January 2018 a pamphlet appeared entitled Busting the Lexit Myths, *edited by Francis Grove-White, with contributions from Catherine West, Nick Donovan, Andy Tarrant, Richard Corbett, Mike Galsworthy, Sarah Veale, Tom Burke and John Monks, and a Foreword by Heidi Alexander and Alison McGovern, published by Open Britain and Labour Campaign for the Single Market.* The Guardian *ran a story on the pamphlet on 30 January, describing it as a call 'on Jeremy Corbyn to stop hiding behind what they call leftwing myths surrounding membership of the European single market after Brexit and instead argue openly about the issue'. The principal arguments were in the papers by Nick Donovan and Andy Tarrant: Donovan claimed that 'other European countries have demonstrated that the existing rules do not prohibit the kind of active industrial strategy that most in the Labour Party would like to see', while Tarrant argued that single-market rules would not prevent a Labour government from renationalising the railways. In addition, both stressed that other international agreements, in particular the World Trade Organisation rules and the European Convention on Human Rights ('which few on the Left advocate leaving' – Tarrant) would equally hamper a Labour government.*

Those of us on the Left who have been opposed to Britain's continued membership of the EU have been motivated by two beliefs. The first and most important of the two is that genuinely left-wing politics has always taken the form of popular action, potentially of a very radical kind. Socialism *is* democracy: when the early followers of Marx called themselves social democrats (for that description was not in its origins an alternative to Marxism but its expression) they knew that achieving full democracy in late nineteenth-century Europe was an essential – indeed *the* essential – condition of socialism. The major achievements of the Left in the twentieth century were the product of highly unconstrained democratic politics, the most striking example being the programme of the Attlee government. Compensation of a kind was paid by the government to the owners of some nationalised industries, but the most striking and longest-lasting instance of nationalisation, the nationalisation of the voluntary hospitals to create the NHS, involved the straightforward expropriation of a form of private property. Whether this was desirable, and what kind of compensation, if any, it was appropriate to pay the owners of the heavy industries, were arguments entirely among the Labour politicians; no law cases attempted to control or reverse the process, nor could they have done so, given the general understanding at the time of the 'omnicompetence' of Parliament. The Labour government was also quite willing to use its democratic mandate to force constitutional change in order to permit its political programme to succeed. We can see this from the Parliament Act of 1949, whose validity, significantly, was not questioned at the time but has since come under scrutiny, a sign of the confidence some lawyers now possess that they can control even Acts passed with the royal assent.

The authors of this pamphlet utterly fail to deal with this issue, which is central to the whole debate on Brexit. Even if the structures of the EU were at the moment entirely friendly to radical socialist measures (which they patently are not), they would be so only as long as a particular political culture existed in the relevant institutions, especially the ECJ. This is a very risky basis for serious political action. There is very little scope for political control over these institutions, even if there were to be a coordinated push across Europe for left-wing policies, of the kind imagined by people like Varoufakis: the EU has been designed to create a strong constitutional order for each country in Europe, administered by independent or quasi-independent agencies. The Left taking power in the EU, it cannot be stressed often enough, would not be like the Left taking power in pre-1973 Britain: however united it would be, without a comprehensive revision of the treaties the current juridical order would persist. Even in the United States, where the power of the Supreme Court and the constraining effects of the Constitution have long been felt, it is possible to introduce some sort of political control over the Court – this is after all why every modern US Presidential election is to a very large extent a campaign about appointments to the Court. But nothing of this kind is conceivable within the EU as currently organised. It is also possible in the US to amend the Constitution, admittedly now with some difficulty; but the EU Constitution, its treaties, can only be changed by unanimous agreement of the member states, something which renders significant amendment almost impossible.

This is a matter of general principle, but the force of the principle is illustrated by the second thing that has led people on the Left to support Brexit. That is the fact that the way the EU constitutional provisions are configured inevitably means, in the circumstances of the modern world, that traditionally socialist measures will find it difficult to pass their scrutiny. As everyone now knows, they are based on the four freedoms of movement within the EU of capital, labour, services and goods, to which one should add a kind of fifth freedom, the freedom of establishment. These 'freedoms' are in turn intended to guarantee a regime of fair competition across Europe: the

EU after all began as a common *market*, and its political structures have all been built around the idea of enforcing competition in cross-border economic activity, and in internal activity in any cases where that activity is open to some degree to external intervention such as foreign investment (which means pretty well everything – even railways, which in the UK at least have only a tenuous physical connection to the rest of Europe). The four freedoms are essentially *market* freedoms. Nineteenth- or early twentieth-century socialists would have perfectly understood what that meant, and how difficult it would be to achieve their ambitions within such a structure.

To see how this can work in practice, let us take a case which the pamphlet does not discuss, but which is of great interest in our present debates. This is the case of *Holship Norge AS v. Norsk Transportarbeiderforbund*, a Norwegian case decided in the EFTA court in April 2016. This was an EFTA case – that is, not directly an ECJ case – but because the rules of the EEA, which the EFTA court administers for the non-EU members of the EEA, require it to acknowledge the four freedoms of the EU as a condition of membership of the single market, the ECJ's jurisprudence effectively determined the result, and the EU Commission was a party to the case. Among other things, this illustrates that the EEA is no solution to the problem of Brexit, at least as viewed from the Left.

The case arose from the fact that since 1976 the Norwegians had operated a dock labour scheme rather like the pre-Thatcher arrangement in Britain, whereby members of the dock workers' union had monopoly rights over unloading cargo from anything other than small craft in Norwegian ports. In 2013 a Danish transport company began to use its own employees to unload its vessels in Norway; the workers were employed by a Norwegian subsidiary of the Danish company, and were unionised, but did not belong to the dock workers' union. The Norwegian dock workers mounted industrial action against them, and the Danish company took the case to the EFTA court. The court ruled against the dock workers' union, and the Norwegian government who supported the union, on two grounds. First, that the freedom of establishment within the EEA meant that any foreign company was entitled to set up in an EEA state; but also, and more far-reachingly, that the general exemption from rules restricting anti-competitive practices which unions possess under EU law – that is, the labour market cannot be entirely a zone of free competition – must be limited. The court concluded, first, that 'to exclude all collective agreements from the reach of competition law would go too far. It would create a legal environment where collective agreements containing provisions restricting competition could be concluded, without there being any judicial review of such restrictions.' And second, that unions could only claim exemption from competition law in matters that affect 'conditions of work and employment', which the court defined as 'wages, working hours and other working conditions. Further elements may concern, *inter alia*, safety, the workplace environment, holidays, training and continuing education, and consultation and co-determination between workers and management ...'.[19] On this basis, they judged that the Norwegian dock labour scheme was illegal, and the Norwegian Supreme Court duly followed the EFTA court's ruling.

This case illustrates exactly the character of the EU. The default principle is free competition, and exceptions have to be justified in a way competition as a principle does not. And in the case of unions, the exceptions are only those of working conditions – the exceptions with which modern liberal capitalists are by and large entirely happy. Any attempt to give unions more power than this, the judgment implies, will be resisted. It is of course the case that many modern social democrats are not unhappy with this kind of ameliorated capitalism, though the idea that the EU is necessary to protect these kinds of workers' rights in a modern state with regular Parliamentary elections is pretty fanciful.

We could make the same sort of point about the issue which has often featured in Lexit discussions, the renationalisation of the British railways. As we know, this is a very popular measure among voters of all political stripes. Andy Tarrant addresses the issue in his section on nationalisation, but he dodges the central question, and in the process reveals exactly the mindset of the authors of this pamphlet. As he concedes, the EU rules *do* preclude a return to the old-style British Railways, as they require free competition in access to the track – in other words, exactly the strange structure introduced by the Major government. There can be nationally owned operating companies, but they have to prove themselves in a free competition for the right to use the infrastructure, unless (a standard proviso in EU jurisprudence) there is some overwhelming public reason against this – which is hardly ever going to be the case in the sense that the ECJ or EFTA courts would recognise. So the present British structure is permitted under EU law, unsurprisingly. But what most people want, a fully integrated publicly owned system (like Amtrak, oddly enough, in the heartland of world capitalism the United States) would be forbidden. The rest of Andy Tarrant's section amounts to little more than telling us we should be glad about this, since the world economy now requires it; this may or may not be true, but it is beside the point, which is whether a perfectly familiar left-wing policy would be impossible within the EU. If it is unwise, let the British people decide on the matter (as they did, for a time, under Thatcher); but if it is not unwise, and circumstances may change and indeed may already have done so, it should not be the case that a whole class of possible policies, most of them part of traditional socialism, should be permanently beyond the pale. As so often in these debates, we see again how the Conservatives, including even Thatcher, should always have supported the EU and the Labour Party should always have opposed it: the EU enshrines in near-perpetuity the capitalism of the 1980s.

28 February 2018

On 26 February 2018, in a speech at Coventry University, Jeremy Corbyn set out what at that point was agreed Labour Party policy towards Brexit. He said the following.

Labour would seek a final deal that gives full access to European markets and maintains the benefits of the single market and the customs union as the Brexit Secretary, David Davis, promised in the House of Commons, with no new impediments to trade and no reduction in rights, standards and protections.

We have long argued that a customs union is a viable option for the final deal. So Labour would seek to negotiate a new comprehensive UK–EU customs union to ensure that there are no tariffs with Europe and to help avoid any need for a hard border in Northern Ireland.

But we are also clear that the option of a new UK customs union with the EU would need to ensure the UK has a say in future trade deals.

A new customs arrangement would depend on Britain being able to negotiate agreement of new trade deals in our national interest.

Labour would not countenance a deal that left Britain as a passive recipient of rules decided elsewhere by others. That would mean ending up as mere rule takers.

No one who is involved in a negotiation starts with the option they really expect to end up with. This is especially true of negotiating with the EU, whose capacity to tangle up not only external parties but also its own members in coils goes far beyond anything even Laocoön experienced. So what are we to make of Jeremy Corbyn's speech on 26 February? As presented, the proposal is not entirely unappealing, though even on its own terms there are many serious objections to it. But as a proposal which, as it stands, will inevitably not actually be implemented, it is largely futile. The only question is, what is likely to be the final destination, if the negotiations start from this point? And would anything short of Corbyn's scheme be acceptable? It is of course quite possible that he and the rest of the Shadow Cabinet are simply being frivolous, and that in reality they do not expect to have to negotiate anything. But it is also possible that the Remainers in the Shadow Cabinet would be quite happy with something well short of what Corbyn outlined, for reasons we shall consider shortly, and – most disturbingly – that they will succeed in getting it.

Corbyn proposes a customs union with the EU. He, and other Labour frontbenchers, have been at pains to stress that this is not the same as entering into the EU's customs union, but instead a new and bilateral agreement between two independent entities. If we take this at face value, it means that both the EU and the UK would have a veto on the tariff arrangements which they collectively reach with the rest of the world. If this were actually to happen, it would therefore not be the same as the deal Turkey has with the EU, whereby it has a (sectoral) customs union with the EU but does not take part in negotiations over external tariffs, merely accepting them as decided by the EU. Instead, it would at least in theory be a union of equals. Leaving aside for the moment the improbability of the EU agreeing to such an arrangement, would it actually be worth having?

In the world of international trade agreements there is a hierarchy. The lowest level of integration is a free-trade area (FTA), such as NAFTA, in which goods move with minimal tariffs between the parties, but each member state can negotiate its own tariffs vis-à-vis non-members. Above this comes a customs union, in which these external tariffs are the same for each member. Above this comes a common market, in which there is regulatory integration, and lastly there is full economic union. If Britain could secure a free-trade agreement with the EU, as Canada has done, would it make any sense to move up to the next level and enter into a customs union? The conventional wisdom is that the principal benefit of a customs union over an FTA comes from the elimination of documentation about the origin of goods crossing frontiers. Goods traded into an member state of an FTA from outside, and then traded on to another member state, have to meet 'rules of origin' requirements, so that appropriate tariffs can be levied on them, while goods produced in the first member state cross the border tariff-free. This happens all the time in an FTA – and will happen in NAFTA even more, now Canada is open to EU goods – and documenting the origin undoubtedly constitutes an annoyance and a cost for importers. But that is the *only* objection to an FTA as compared to a customs union, and it pales into insignificance when set against the many political objections to a customs union.

NAFTA in fact provides us with an excellent example of this, since Canadian economists and politicians periodically discussed the merits of turning NAFTA into a customs union (this was before the days of Trump). As a result, they had to think hard about precisely the question of the merits of a customs union over an FTA. Though almost everyone concerned agreed that eliminating the need to document origin would be an economic advantage, they disagreed about how much the savings would be, with some saying that it would be trivial. And many of them, especially on the Left, quickly concluded that the political disadvantages clearly outweighed the small economic benefit. This has also been the position taken in practice by Canadian governments, who have not sought to persuade the US to upgrade NAFTA into a customs union. A customs union between the relatively small Canada and the much larger US would obviously tend to favour international arrangements which were in the interests of the United States; could the Canada–EU FTA have been achieved if the negotiations had had to involve America? Exactly the same would be true even of the kind of UK–EU customs union Corbyn is hoping for.

Defenders of Corbyn's proposal say that it would solve the problem of the Irish border after Brexit. Again, it is true that it would eliminate some paperwork, but at a high price in terms of the wider political implications. Trade across the US–Canada border flows pretty freely without a customs union: car manufactures, for example, have fully integrated production in plants on both sides of the border. No one in Britain is proposing to end the common travel area which is in effect a passport union between Great Britain and the Republic, so (unlike in the US) there would need be very little policing of individuals crossing the border; non-Irish EU citizens using an open border to settle in the UK would be like the many non-EU citizens currently overstaying their visas, etc., in the UK, and not a new or special problem. And anyway, a customs union would make no difference to this.

However, all of this is academic, since there is no possibility of Corbyn's proposal actually being implemented. This is not to say that Corbyn could not be the person leading negotiations with the EU, but simply (as I said at the beginning) that the first move in a negotiation cannot be the one the parties end up with. So anything which a Corbyn government might agree to would have to be worse than what he outlined on 26 February. If his proposal is not especially attractive as it stands, why would anyone settle for something worse? One answer to this question might be that it would be the equivalent of virtue signalling: something which has no intrinsic merit might be supported because of the message it sends about political allegiance. This is no doubt true for some advocates of the proposal, but there is another and more troubling possibility.

A lesser version of the Corbyn proposal which could be agreed on would be broadly similar to the current EU–Turkey arrangement. Only this, in fact, is possible, since there is no other concession which could be made in the course of negotiations by a Corbyn government which genuinely wanted to be in a customs union. The key feature of this arrangement is that only the EU negotiates external tariffs; and this, it is paradoxical to say, might be the real reason why certain British politicians would be keen on it – in some ways keener than on the Corbyn proposal. The unusual customs union with Turkey came about because it was supposed that at some point in the relatively near future Turkey would become a member of the EU, and would then be fully involved in setting tariffs, etc. It was not supposed that Turkey would be a rule taker in perpetuity. And if Britain were to enter into an arrangement of this kind, it is not hard to see what the result would be. After a few years, it would be said that it was unsustainable, and that Britain had to choose between leaving the customs union and moving back into the institutions which decide policy. Given public exhaustion over the issues, a campaign from business urging us to be able to 'have a say' over our economic future, and (probably) a disinclination to hold a referendum on the question, the outcome is easy to predict. In other words, the proposal to enter 'a' customs union is primarily a trap, set by people who basically wish to re-enter the EU.

One of the tragedies, if Labour does decide to propose a customs union, is that a year and a half ago the party endorsed a perfectly well-judged critique of doing so. At the party conference in September 2016, Barry Gardiner, currently the shadow trade secretary (and once described in *The Guardian* as 'one of the best educated and most internationally experienced MPs'), set out his vision of a 'Just Trading Community'. This was in turn endorsed in the Labour manifesto for the general election of 2017. In his speech to the conference, Gardiner said the following.

> For too long governments and politicians have allowed for one-way trade deals to be concluded behind closed doors on terms that give foreign investors power to sue governments if they believe that laws and policies may affect their profit potential – even if those laws are passed in the public interest.
>
> Deals like TTIP have struggled to find any support amongst the public because of the dangerous risk to sovereignty and because people do not believe that anybody other than big business benefits from them.
>
> That is why, today at Labour Party Conference, I have announced the launch of the Just Trading Community, bringing together like-minded politicians and legislators to work towards establishing a new model trade agreement that places, at its very heart, the protection, promotion and progression of workers' rights, human rights, quality standards and environmental safeguards.
>
> Labour knows that small and medium-sized businesses are the backbone of this economy and yet they are too often ignored when it comes to negotiating international trade deals and in receiving the support necessary to expand into new export markets.
>
> That is why I have also announced today that any future trade deal under a Labour government would incorporate a mandatory requirement that any country who wants to sign a trade agreement with the UK must set out a strategy for supporting our SMEs seeking to export to them.

This entire vision would be rendered pointless if Britain were to enter into a customs union with any other countries. But Gardiner spoke for many on the Left, echoing for example the opposition to TTIP which in part fuelled Bernie Sanders' campaign in America. If the party does repudiate this vision and return to its posture under Blair – vaguely hoping that left-wing measures might some day be adopted by the EU while accepting in practice the very different kinds of measure which actually emanate from its decision-making institutions – it will have cut its ties with the genuinely radical forces on the Left, and in the end it will not even gain any electoral advantage from having done so.

9 March 2018

On 2 March 2018 Theresa May gave a speech on 'our future economic partnership with the European Union'. Originally supposed to have been given at Newcastle – the epicentre of the 'Leave' vote – it was all too appropriately rescheduled for the Mansion House in London, as a result of 'bad weather'.

All major political speeches work by including the most important material in an apparently reasonable, almost throwaway fashion. This was certainly true of Theresa May's speech in London on 2 March. The most significant passage was the following.

> If we want good access to each other's markets, it has to be on fair terms. As with any trade agreement, we must accept the need for binding commitments – for example, we may choose to commit some areas of our regulations like state aid and competition to remaining in step with the EU's.
>
> The UK drove much of the policy in this area and we have much to gain from maintaining proper disciplines on the use of subsidies and on anti-competitive practices. Furthermore, as I said in Florence, we share the same set of fundamental beliefs; a belief in free trade, rigorous and fair competition, strong consumer rights, and that trying

to beat other countries' industries by unfairly subsidising one's own is a serious mistake.

As far as I can tell, not many commentators nor prominent Brexiteers have leaped onto these remarks. Indeed, the most high-profile figure to do so was Jeremy Corbyn, in his response to May in Parliament on 5 March, when he said that 'The Prime Minister's only clear priority seems to be to tie the UK permanently to EU rules that have been used to enforce privatisation and block support for industry.'

The reasons for this relative neglect tell us a lot about the strange history of Britain's relationship with the EU. From the beginning it was clear that a jurisprudence based on the innocuous-sounding 'four freedoms' was in fact going to entrench a certain kind of competitive capitalism in each member state, since large-scale political intervention in the economy would almost certainly be ruled illegal. This was already obvious to the members of Harold Wilson's Cabinet when they met at Chequers in 1966 to discuss whether they should keep Macmillan's failed application to join the EEC on the table or withdraw it and seek other options. Tommy Balogh urged instead a North Atlantic Free Trade Area, and he was broadly supported in his opposition to the EEC by the other leading economic advisors to the Treasury, Nicky Kaldor and Robert Neild. Though the Wilson Cabinet decided to keep the application alive, largely as a means of underpinning Britain's post-imperial ambitions, the unhappiness of Labour with the European project had been made quite clear.

The unhappiness continued down to the mid-1980s. Labour whipped against the final vote on the European Communities Act in 1972 – which passed, certain current Remainers agitating for a second referendum should be reminded, by a majority of only seventeen, and the second reading had earlier passed by a still smaller majority, of eight. Our entire history of membership of the EU would have been different had *five* members of the Commons voted differently on the second reading on 17 February 1972; Hansard recorded that the members voting for the second and third readings included Norman Tebbit, Nicholas Ridley and 'the Rt. Hon. Mrs Margaret Thatcher'. In government, as we know, Wilson solved the dilemma of whether to pull out by instituting the first referendum in British history, and allowing a free vote on it to his Cabinet; but even after Leave lost the 1975 vote, Labour remained largely hostile to the EEC. A party conference the same year had voted two-to-one to leave, and it became official policy to do so in 1981, precipitating the split in the party and the formation of the SDP by prominent pro-Europeans – a split which arguably undermined Labour's authority and permitted Thatcher's landslide victory in 1983. In that election Labour polled 8.5 million and the Lib/SDP Alliance 7.7 million, as against Thatcher's 13 million. Another road not taken: suppose the SDP leaders had remained loyal to their party, Thatcher might well have lost in 1983. Her regime would not then have seemed the inevitable turning-point in history which to many people it subsequently appeared to be – including to Tony Blair. We could say without much exaggeration that Thatcher was the principal – and ungrateful – beneficiary of Britain's membership of the EEC.

The positions the two parties took up prior to the mid-1980s were thus entirely in line with the logic of the EEC. Tories correctly saw it as a way of locking Britain into structures which essentially precluded the kind of socialism which was still the aim of the Labour Party in the 1960s and 1970s, while the Labour Party (though not all its politicians) correctly saw it in exactly the same light. Those of us who support Brexit today, from the perspective of either the Right or the Left, do so (I think it would be fair to say) very much because we do not believe in *any* structures which lock people into particular political policies in near-perpetuity. But we should remember that it was the Tories who originally chose to use this weapon against their opponents, and Labour who were willing to have a fair fight, and to run the risk that in the future a Tory government might overturn their socialist measures. One is reminded of Harold Laski's famous quip, that 'the gentlemen of England will always play the game, but they reserve the right to change the rules'.

From the mid-1980s onwards this fundamental logic was obscured, first by Labour's decision to accept membership (though as we know this was never whole-hearted) and second by the turn against the EU on the part of many Tories, including Thatcher herself. The full reasons for this swapping of positions remain (to my mind at least) rather unclear, since the realities of the EEC/EU had not substantially changed; but on the eve of the referendum we suddenly discovered that the Labour Party was now being led by people who had always understood the logic of the EU, and had not after all changed their position on it. Whatever his faults, Brexiteers of all stripes owe a considerable debt to Corbyn, who (like Bernie Sanders in America) emerged from relative obscurity to utter political sentiments which had been treated as outlandish for thirty years or more. Acute Conservative commentators also began to remember why their party had once been the prime mover behind Britain's entry into the EEC; one of the most acute, Charles Moore, asked in June last year:

> Could the EU prevent a government led by Jeremy Corbyn? Since our confusing general election result last month, I find significant numbers of people asking this question. Such people do not like Mr Corbyn. Indeed, they regard a government led by him as the worst of all the imaginable possibilities facing our country. It spooks them because, before June 8, they had considered it all but unimaginable. They tend to think that if the EU could keep Mr Corbyn out, perhaps we had better stay in.
>
> They are not wrong to raise this question. In the now largely forgotten days when most Conservatives were strongly pro-European, the threat of the hard Left helped explain why ...

In a Britain dominated by strikes, 'Europe' beckoned. The EEC was scarcely a paragon of free-market virtue, but it seemed to offer relative industrial peace. Right-wing Labour supporters thought it could marginalise the extremists. A lot of Tories thought decent, free, bourgeois Britain was finished. Perhaps Brussels could rescue it ...

It probably is true that a Corbyn government could be much more easily beaten down with Britain in the EU than outside it. His socialism-in-one-country would quickly fall foul of single market rules and be squashed by the commission (Brussels) and the European Court of Justice (Luxembourg) ...[20]

To his enormous credit, Moore resisted the temptation to look to the EU for protection against a Corbyn government, stating clearly that it must not be the case that it should be 'virtually unconstitutional for there to be a Labour government'; but his article was one of the few I have read which recognised the fundamental issues at play in the last forty years of British politics.

And this is now the key issue to be resolved in Britain's so-called 'negotiations' with the EU over our future relationship with the European Union. What May let slip on 2 March was that the Tories still want to use the EU as a means of blocking Corbyn-style politics in perpetuity. They will now not do it through membership of the EU, at least at the moment, but they will do it through something equally effective and without any of the EU's irksome baggage, namely a 'binding commitment' to just those aspects of EU membership which prevent effective socialist measures within Britain.

It is no surprise that Corbyn spotted this, given his familiarity with this history, and also no surprise that Tory Brexiteers (who still dominate the Brexit debate) kept quiet about it. But the urgent question is whether Corbyn and the Labour Party can do anything to stop it. Technically speaking, the commitment they have recently entered into to join a customs union with the EU does not entail these kinds of institutional constraints on state aid, etc.;

but a customs union even of the kind they are officially endorsing – that is, a bilateral arrangement between the EU and the UK, rather than simple membership of the EU's customs union – puts a great deal of British domestic politics potentially under a juridical regime which is likely to insist on uniformity in market behaviour across the customs union, in order to prevent competitive gaming of the customs regime by the countries involved. Once one is in structures of this kind in the modern world they tend to move in only one direction; this was at the heart of Sanders' opposition to the TPP and TTIP. It is true that membership of the WTO imposes certain constraints on what governments can do with regard to political intervention in the economy, but the constraints are far less than (for example) those imposed on its members by the EU, since they refer exclusively to interventions which affect external trade. A full-scale renationalisation of the British railways would encounter no problems from the WTO, but would at the least have to be defended in front of the ECJ if Britain were still to be in the EU.[21] The difficulty with Labour's current proposal is that even if (miraculously) it were to be accepted as it stands, we have no idea what it is going to look like once the administrative and judicial institutions get going on it, but we have no grounds whatsoever for optimism. And, of course, it will not be accepted as it stands.

Corbyn's leadership of the Labour Party has offered the chance of breaking out of the straitjacket into which the EU has strapped all the political parties of Europe. As we can see in country after country on the Continent, it is the old left-wing parties which have been the chief victims of this straitjacket. They have all suffered from the inability of their leaders to renounce their old allegiance to the European project, and it is no accident that the new left-wing parties such as Syriza which have begun to fill the gap left by the electoral implosion of the old parties are almost all in varying degrees opposed to the EU. The British Labour Party is at the moment the one exception to this rule, and at times in the recent past it has come perilously close to succumbing to the same fate as its Continental equivalents. Corbyn's remarks on 5 March show that at some level he understands this, and it will be tragedy of historic dimensions if he allows himself to be forced back into the straitjacket by timorous (or worse) colleagues in the Shadow Cabinet.

11 April 2018

For a symposium at the LSE on 13 April 2018, on 'The Political Theory of Brexit: Alternative Perspectives' (which was the origin of the Full Brexit group), I wrote a short paper for a panel on 'Sovereignty'. This is a longer version of the paper.

One of the commonest arguments against Brexit from those whose politics in general I sympathise with is that the ideal of regaining power over our own legal arrangements is a fantasy. Every modern state is so thoroughly enmeshed in a series of international arrangements that it can never be free in the old, nineteenth-century sense. Why bother with the elaborate and difficult business of leaving the EU, when we will simply have to accommodate ourselves to the WTO, and to the European and UN Conventions on Human Rights? Another version of this argument, which I also respect, is that it is not possible to have 'socialism in one country' – it is impossible in practice to cut oneself off from the global economy, and one has to bend to its demands, or turn oneself into Cuba. If that means that one cannot have socialism as it was understood before the 1980s, too bad. This is sometimes said with that special *frisson* which people feel when they think they are being realistic in the face of other people's romanticism – though realism of this kind is really a form of romance itself.

As I said, this is an argument I respect, and we have to take it seriously. One easy, but I think fallacious, response to it is that none of these other international arrangements reach into the very heart of our common life and its juridical character as the EU and the ECJ do. But that is, I think, to misunderstand the actual character of the relationship between the member states and the EU. As I have now argued in a number of places, the best way of theorising about that relationship is not to suppose that the EU is a kind of state, or has the ambition to become one: the disclaimers issued by the Eurocrats are to this extent correct. Nor is it true that the member states have lost their sovereignty, in the sense of *state* sovereignty. Each one remains a *state* in the sense that it is the ultimate authority for its citizens, and possesses that standing vis-à-vis other states in the international sphere; no EU state is going to renounce its seat at the United Nations. What the structures of the EU are is best understood as a *coordinated constitutional order* for each state. The member states voted severally to impose a series of constraints on what their domestic legislatures could do, constraints which stand in relation to the legislatures exactly as their domestic constitutions (in all countries except Britain) do. This is what is really meant by the annoying term 'pooling sovereignty', something which on most reasonable accounts cannot be done. I should observe here that the British have found it hard to understand or adjust to a system of this kind since they had no experience before 1973 of constitutional constraints of this sort *at all*. For countries which had had them for a century or more, adding the EU was not such a dramatic act as it was for the UK, and it is no coincidence that when Wilson came back into power he felt that the new arrangements had to be legitimated by something else which was a novelty for Britain, namely a plebiscite, the commonest means in the rest of the world of legitimating constitutions which constrain the legislatures.

The authority of the EU constraints comes from the original vote to impose them, just as the old constitutions' authority did, and still does; and the state can simply vote to nullify the EU constraints, as it can those of its other constitutional instruments. But there are two differences between the EU and the old domestic constitutions. One is that the site of interpretation is partly outside the country, though from the point of view of the relationship between the legislature and the constitutional constraints this is actually a rather trivial difference, particularly given the cultural similarity between jurists from different countries. The really important difference is not often emphasised: it is that the EU constitutional constraints have to be accepted *as a package*. Most constitutions can be amended without having to be entirely rejected – though some have tried to build in barriers to amendment in fundamental respects, such as Norway, Greece, Portugal and, above all, Germany. But the EU, as we are discovering, is not like that: if a member state doesn't like some feature, in particular the implications of some judgment at the ECJ, it cannot do what it would do for other constitutional laws and *change* them, at least not without going into an elaborate and probably impossible set of international negotiations. This renders the EU structures far more rigid than any other juridical constraints on domestic legislatures, except perhaps in Germany, and gives the constitutional court enormous power over all the member states. It must be emphasised that this is not a problem peculiar to Britain, though as I said the British were unusual in being wholly unaccustomed to such a state of affairs.

When people in Britain talk about the 'loss of sovereignty' implicit in membership of the EU, what they principally have in mind, I believe, is the fact that *democratic* sovereignty is impeded in this fashion – that is, the *democratic* will cannot change important features of the politics of the country. And when this complaint is heard with bafflement on the Continent and by some of the ruling class in this country, it is because in the other sense of sovereignty – the ultimate independence of a 'state' as a juridical entity – there has in the end been no such loss. There is a long and interesting history of the difference between these two senses which I do not want to talk about today, but which I would simply summarise by saying that what we might call the 'hypostasisation' of the state, treating it as a person, has always been used as a way of constraining the late eighteenth- and nineteenth-century push towards democracy – the push, that is, based on the belief that the people currently living under a particular political regime have the full power to change it, and should not be 'ruled by the dead', as Bentham put it in the most powerful attack on undemocratic constitutionalising ever penned.[22]

Seen from this perspective, the formal character of a constitutional rule is not really the issue. What matters is the extent to which as a matter of fact it is part of a large package which has to be changed as a whole, thereby introducing a set of powerful disincentives to change which are not intrinsic to the issue under consideration. For example, we might want to thoroughly renationalise the railways. This looks as if it should be a stand-alone question; but the legal power to do so is dependent on a judgment from the ECJ about whether such a policy would be anti-competitive, and if the judgment were to go against the policy, the only way to overturn it would be through a renegotiation of the treaties setting up the EU, or pulling out of it altogether. Compare what would happen without the EU; indeed, think about what the Attlee government *did* do, with no legal barriers to its programme. This is true whether or not we think that the ECJ would rule against nationalisation, though as a matter of fact I think it is pretty clear that at least it would not countenance an Attlee-style programme.

A judgment of the ECJ is directly applicable in the UK in a way that (say) the rulings of the UN Human Rights Committees are not, or the rulings of the European Court of Human Rights (ECtHR) before the incorporation of the European Convention in British law in 1998 were not, and some leftish Brexiteers find comfort in this: once we are out of the EU we will be in a position to control our own laws, and the other international arrangements which supporters of Britain's membership point to as no different from the EU do not have the same legal status within the UK. But I think this is to put too much weight on the *forms*, and is not really an answer to the Remainers' challenge. If there is a substantial price to be paid internationally for the adoption of a particular policy, then the policy is no longer stand-alone, whatever the legal forms may be. *In extremis* Parliament can ignore or rebut any of these rulings, but extraneous considerations have been introduced into its deliberations just as they have in the case of the EU. The idea that it can always take action and that we are therefore freer than we are in the EU rests, as I have said, on a misunderstanding of the actual character of our membership of the EU, for in that respect too we can always take action. In both cases the cost of the action has been rendered artificially high, however, just as constitutionalising a policy domestically renders it far harder to change than an ordinary piece of legislation – though international agreements of this kind make their provisions even harder to change than a single article of a domestic constitution would be. Treaties of any kind always play *some* role in the domestic judicial process in Britain; roughly, the presumption is that they are to be honoured and applied unless Parliament has clearly ruled against doing so. So given what I have said about the packaged character of these agreements, I am not sure that the real difference between (say) the ECHR before 1998 and the ECHR after 1998 is all that great. When the ECtHR produced a decision on an important case in 1983 which effectively destroyed the old closed-shop agreements in the UK, they awarded damages to the petitioners which the then British government had to pay (gladly, of course, given that it was the Thatcher government at the time), and required the government to report on how it was bringing domestic legislation into line (which it also gladly complied with). The Court's role in breaking union power in the Thatcher years seems all but forgotten.

So what is to be done? I think the way forward is to think more carefully about the concrete character of the principal international agreements, and to distinguish between them. The examples I want to use are, first, the earliest such agreement to have clear implications for domestic law, namely the section of the Versailles Treaty setting up the International Labour Organisation; and, second, the European Convention on Human Rights. The first was created by socialists, or at least the Left, and reluctantly acceded to by the Right; the second was created by the Right, and reluctantly acceded to by the Left. Their different characters give us suggestions about how the Left should think about international arrangements. The modern Left in Britain has rather lost interest in the ILO and seems to be rather keen on the European Convention, but this is an error comparable to its similar error over the EU.

During the First World War it was widely felt that (as the General Secretary of the General Federation of Trades Unions said in a letter to Asquith in 1916):

> Nearly all other wars have ended with treaties which conserved the rights of kings, the boundaries of nations and the privileges of property. The poor people have had no part in the making of war or peace; they have suffered, they have endured contumely, and they have died, but never yet has monarch or statesman made their situation a determining factor in a treaty of peace.[23]

In July 1916 there was a meeting of trades unionists from the Allied countries at Leeds, followed by one from neutral countries and the 'Central Powers', i.e. the allies of Germany, in October 1917 at Berne, to discuss what such a treaty should include. The relative extent of coordination between the parties who were still involved in a ferocious war is very striking, as is the assumption on both sides that there would be an extensive peace treaty.[24] Obvious issues were work conditions and trades union rights, though high up the agenda of both conferences, interestingly from our current perspective, was the issue of freedom of movement. Each conference endorsed the general principle that (in the words of the Leeds Resolutions): 'Every workman, no matter to which nationality he may belong, ought to have the right to work wherever he can find employment';[25] but they also qualified this by prescribing various restrictions on immigration, including the banning of contract labour recruited overseas with a view to avoiding labour agreements in the host country.[26] Surprisingly to our eyes, the trades unionists were more concerned with guaranteeing freedom of *emigration*: by 1914 a number of countries had begun to consider restrictions on emigration, with a particularly draconian law to that effect passed in Hungary in 1909, all largely aimed at curtailing emigration to the United States.

These concerns all found their way into the articles of the Versailles Peace Treaty setting up the ILO (along, interestingly, with the 'principle that men and women should receive equal remuneration for work of equal value') (Article 427). But they were not (at first) configured as a declaration of rights. Instead, each member state undertook to 'at the earliest practicable moment ... bring [any] recommendation or draft convention [from the ILO] before the authority or authorities within whose competence the matter lies, for the enactment of legislation or other action', so that each measure was treated separately and could be accepted or rejected individually. If a 'convention', as distinct from the lesser category of a 'recommendation', was legislated for, there were restrictions on whether it could be repealed without some action being taken by other countries which had ratified the convention, usually economic sanctions of some kind, the idea being that poor labour conditions were a form of unfair trade.[27] The treaty prescribed a period of ten years before a convention which had been ratified could be (to use the technical term) 'denounced' by a member country without such a retaliation; if it was not denounced during the year following the expiration of the first ten-year period, it could not be denounced for another ten years, and so on. In doing so, it was modelling its conventions on commercial treaties which for many years had contained such clauses permitting unilateral denunciation within a defined time period.

The Versailles Treaty had thus created a body which was entitled to make rules governing the domestic economy of member states, and by doing so had introduced a new kind of legislation into domestic politics. It is true that initially the ILO was significantly circumscribed, since, first, each resolution had to be separately agreed by a member state if it was to have any effect on its internal policies, and, second, even if a convention was ratified by a member state, it could be unilaterally denounced after ten years without a member state having to leave the Organisation – each convention was in effect a treaty between individual members of the ILO. The Thatcher government indeed denounced three conventions which in its view restricted the labour market in the UK, two of which had been ratified by the Attlee government.[28]

But the men of the Left who created the ILO were extremely wary of anything like a supranational authority. The left-wing German republican government in 1919 proposed the creation of a body whose rulings on labour issues would automatically have the force of international law, but they were rebuffed by the other parties in the negotiations. As Clemenceau put it with characteristic brutality: 'The Allied and Associated Democracies, who have had a very long experience of democratic institutions', understand that 'the workers of one country are not prepared to be bound in all matters by laws imposed on them by representatives of other countries; international conventions ... are therefore ... more effective than international labour laws.'[29] As these founders understood, the ability which their scheme gave a Thatcher to denounce conventions was a *quid pro quo* for having them in the first place – and they would have realised that Blair could have reinstated them for another ten years, had he so wished. That he did not do so is a particularly good example of the way he hid behind Thatcher's skirts.

In 1998 there was an attempt to bring the ILO more in line with what was by then becoming an international norm, when the 'Declaration on Fundamental Principles and Rights at Work' was adopted at the 86th International Labour Conference. But this Declaration, although in theory binding all member states *as a condition of membership* to accept a set of basic principles (including no gender discrimination in pay), did not invoke the enforcement mechanism written into the 1919 treaty for individual conventions, and though the ILO subsequently nominated eight existing conventions as in accordance with the Declaration, it left their original juridical status unaltered. So it is probable – though this has never been put to the test – that if a country were to denounce one of them, it would be able to remain a member of the ILO, just as it could have done earlier.

There have been some powerful criticisms of the Declaration from people on the Left, including Guy Standing, who have argued that it was a retrogressive step, since it diverted attention from the concrete work of the ILO and introduced a set of vaguely worded 'rights' which were perfectly acceptable to a neoliberal globalising world – unlike the conventions which the Thatcher government had denounced, as the very act of denunciation testifies. Immigration, for example, which had been uppermost in the minds of the original founders of the ILO, disappeared from the Declaration on Fundamental Principles. And like all such sets of rights, if it had been justiciable, it would have been applied to a very wide range of cases, constituting precisely the 'package' of which I spoke earlier.

The ILO was the product of European socialists working together, well aware that they needed full democracy at home in order to introduce their measures. In this respect it stands in sharp contrast to my other example, the European Convention on Human Rights. Though the Convention is now frequently praised from a leftish perspective, its origins, as Marco Duranti has recently documented in an important and path-breaking book,[30] lie squarely in post-war anxiety to constrain not merely Eastern European communism but Western European socialism as well. In fact, the tendentious modern history of the Convention is itself a revealing example of how the old Left has been marginalised in today's world.

The movement for it began in an independent 'Congress of Europe' organised at The Hague in May 1948 by the Joint International Committee for the Movements for European Unity, with its star attraction being Winston Churchill, who was of course by then only the leader of the Opposition in Britain. The Congress called for the drafting of a convention of human rights and a court to enforce them, a call which was then considered by the Council of Europe, founded in May of the following year. The Convention on Human Rights was the first convention it issued, after the conventions setting up the Council itself; it was opened for signature in November 1950. But more or less forgotten until Duranti's book has been the fact that from the beginning the project was bitterly opposed by the European Left, particularly in Britain.

The Labour Party described the Congress of Europe as a project of 'reactionary politicians', and persuaded the Socialist Conference on European Policy meeting at Paris to bar any member of a socialist party executive committee from attending it.[31] David Maxwell Fyfe – frequently (and correctly) invoked in the modern literature on the Convention as one of its principal progenitors, mostly nowadays in a transparent attempt to give it some legitimate British ancestry for a sceptical public in the UK – was a thoroughgoing Conservative and former appeaser who described the Labour government's nationalisation of steel as 'a step on the road towards totalitarian government in England', and called for 'an overhaul of the relations between the law-making body and the judicial tribunals' to prevent the emergence of 'the legal structure of a totalitarian dictatorship'.[32] In the Consultative Assembly debating the proposed Convention, he explicitly compared the European human rights court to the US Supreme Court, something which caused Arwyn Ungoed-Thomas, a Welsh Labour MP, to respond that the Supreme Court had sought to overturn the New Deal on the flimsiest of pretexts, and that the draft Convention was 'anti-democratic and reactionary'.[33]

When the Attlee Cabinet considered the draft Convention in August 1950, Stafford Cripps launched a comprehensive and well-judged attack on the whole idea:

> The Chancellor of the Exchequer said that a Government committed to the policy of a planned economy could not ratify this Convention on Human Rights. He drew attention to various Articles in the draft Convention, e.g., on powers of entry into private premises, which were inconsistent with the powers of economic control which were essential to the operation of a planned economy. The Convention had originally been conceived as a statement of the rights which western civilisation preserved for the individual, in contrast to the absence of such rights in Communist-dominated countries; but, if the Convention were adopted in its present form, this country could be pilloried for infractions of its provisions which would be unavoidable in the course of economic planning. The draft Convention would be acceptable only to those who believed in a free economy and a minimum amount of State intervention in economic affairs.[34]

The most objectionable clauses in the proposed Convention, from the point of view of the Left, were those guaranteeing a right to private property and the right of parents to have their children educated in accordance with their own religious beliefs. The former was common ground for all the socialist parties of Europe, since they all understood the impediment it would represent to their economic policies, while the latter was of particular concern to the secularist parties on the French Left; it was a 'right' which the Catholic Church had repeatedly tried to insert into the French Constitution, so far without success. Socialist delegates from across Europe to the Council of Europe's Consultative Assembly succeeded in getting both clauses dropped from the final draft of the Convention which was approved in late 1950 and ratified by the Attlee government during its precarious second term; though France, where the Legislative Assembly had been dominated by the Left including the Communists (the largest party in both votes and seats) since November 1946, refused to ratify – and indeed did not do so until 1974, something often forgotten in the modern hagiography of the Convention.

However, in a moment of far-reaching significance, property and education clauses were reinserted in the first protocol to the Convention in March 1952. The Attlee government gave up trying to veto their insertion, but managed to head off the demand from most other delegates that the property clause should require compensation for any nationalisation by a member state. Revealingly, however, the ECtHR, in a 1986 court case arising from the Wilson government's nationalisation of shipbuilding, ruled that despite this history the property clause must imply a right to fair compensation. So all the Attlee government's diplomacy in the end came to nothing.

While the property clause divided British politicians, with those on the Right pushing for it precisely to discourage nationalisation without compensation, almost all of them were agreed on resisting Article 25, which allowed individual petition to the Court of Human Rights, and which almost all the other countries favoured. The Attlee Cabinet was clear on the subject; in the same meeting at which Stafford Cripps delivered his withering attack on the draft,

> Ministers agreed that, if individuals had a right to take alleged infractions of the Convention from the courts of

this country to a European Court of Human Rights, the
effect on the judicial system of this country might be very
serious. It was intolerable that the code of common law
and statute law which had been built up in this country
over many years should be made subject to review by an
International Court administering no defined system of
law ...

British diplomacy could do nothing, however, in the face
of the near-universal acceptance of this clause, and the
Labour government's only recourse was to ratify the
Convention with a reservation excluding both Article 25
and Article 46, covering the jurisdiction of the Court as a
whole.

This stance was preserved by succeeding Conservative
administrations, but it was abandoned in 1966 by the
Wilson government, which thereby opened up the steady
increase in the Court's involvement in British affairs
which has repeatedly caused disquiet in the UK. The
1966 decision was potentially very far-reaching, but it
was arrived at with no discussion in Cabinet, and in a
spirit of frivolity – Gerald Gardiner, the Lord Chancellor,
pronounced, 'I do think that this would cost us nothing
and would show that a Labour government is not anti-
Europe as such.'[35] It was of course a gesture by the Wilson
government at the start of its awkward attempt to keep on
the table the application to join the EEC which had been
rebuffed in 1963 by de Gaulle, and it appears to have been
treated as a trivial part of the much more complicated
question of EEC membership. It is true that between 1966
and 1998, when the Blair government passed the Human
Rights Act, the ECtHR's judgments even on individual
petitions had no direct effect in the UK, in the sense that
any action brought before the ECtHR was against the
UK government and not a domestic defendant; but the
difference between 1966 and 1998 can be exaggerated,
as I have already said. The common claim that the issue
of the EU and the issue of the ECHR are separate is not

in fact true: without an intention to join the EU, one can reasonably suppose, the Wilson government would have maintained the reservations entered into by their predecessors.

The EU was of course created by the same sort of people who created the ECHR, and the Attlee government's response to its first institutional expression, the Coal and Steel Community, was broadly similar to its response to the ECHR. I do not now want to go into the question of how thoroughly 'neoliberal' the EU currently is, but I would just say that the dangers implicit in its character were obvious from the beginning. Addressing an audience at Colchester in July 1950, John Strachey, the Minister of War, said:

> What is the real issue underlying the Schuman Plan? This is a plan to give control of the coal and steel industries of Europe ... into the hands of a council of eight or nine men. These men were to have complete power of these industries and they were not to be responsible to any Government or Parliament or other democratic body. These dictators, responsible to no one but themselves, were to have power ... to close down half of the coal mines in South Wales or the steel mills of Sheffield if they thought fit – and if they thought it would profit the shareholders of these industries to do so ...
>
> Is it not perfectly obvious that the real purpose was precisely to put up a barrier against the control of the basic industries of Europe by the European people. After all, gradually and with difficulty ... the people of Europe and the people of Britain are getting hold of economic power ...
>
> All this is an alarm bell to the great capitalist interests of Europe. Therefore they put up this sort of plan by which the real power in these industries is put in the hands of an irresponsible international body free from all democratic control ...
>
> We shall get more and more of these schemes no doubt, which under the guise of internationalism are designed to prevent the people really controlling their economic system.[36]

These dangers became even more obvious after the Treaty of Rome formalised the 'four freedoms', and they were eloquently captured in an article by Nye Bevan in August 1957.

> In the absence of a wider sovereignty, all the conception of a common market does is to elevate the market place to the status now enjoyed by various European parliaments. It is at this point that Socialists become suspicious of what is intended. Is it the disfranchisement of the people and the enfranchisement of market forces? Are we now expected to go back almost a century, reject socialism and clasp free trade to our bosoms as though it were the one solution of our social evils? ... The conception of a Common Market for Europe ... is the result of a political malaise following upon the failure of Socialists to use the sovereign power of their parliaments to plan their economic life.
>
> It is an escapist conception in which the play of market forces will take the place of political responsibility ... Socialists cannot at one and the same time call for economic planning and accept the verdict of free competition, no matter how extensive the area it covers. The jungle is not made more acceptable just because it is almost limitless ...[37]

I am not sure I can add anything to this.

26 April 2018:
Why Is Everyone So
Hysterical About Brexit?

Everyone who has been involved in the Brexit debates since the referendum was called has been conscious of the viciousness of the campaign. The Scottish referendum should have prepared us for it, but nevertheless it came as a shock to many of us that old friendships could be broken and adult tears shed over what many people had thought was a rather technical issue. I have been voting in every British election since 1970, and I do not remember any period – even the Three Day Week and the Miners' Strike – in which so many people felt free to voice such venomous denunciations of their political opponents. This is partly because the tribes of British politics have become much more closed to one another, and it came as a shock to their members that in the world outside there was such widespread disagreement with their views; this was particularly so in the British universities, where the old Tory professors who were still quite thick on the ground in the 1970s have almost entirely disappeared. But this was not the fundamental reason for the venom, and under-standing what the fundamental reason was takes us into the heart of the debate about Brexit.

Like the Scottish referendum, the Brexit referendum put a constitutional question to the electorate. This has often been ignored or misunderstood, largely because the British have until recently never had to think about what it might mean. It is, for example, often asserted that unlike most of the world Britain has an 'unwritten' constitution. This is not in fact true, since there is a whole set of Parliamentary statutes which together specify most fundamental features of British political life, including the Bill of Rights, the Act of Union, the Act of Settlement, the Parliament Act, the European Communities Act, and so on. What differentiates these written laws from the written laws that form, for example, the American Constitution is that in Britain they are passed by the same body which passes ordinary legislation of the most trivial kind: there is no separate procedure, as there is now in most countries, for passing constitutional laws in some way other than the processes of ordinary legislation.

Since the American and French revolutions, these separate procedures have been widely adopted because they have been seen as more purely democratic than the means by which day-to-day legislation is enacted. The most obvious example of this is the referendum, which was used by many states immediately after the American Revolution to ground their new state constitutions, and which was used throughout the revolutionary years in France to legitimate the new regimes. The referendum was never universally adopted for this purpose, and the Federal Constitution in the US was not ratified through a national plebiscite, though it was ratified through a different and more democratic set of institutions than the existing governments of the individual states; but by now a large number of modern nations treat the referendum as the natural means of constitutional legislation.

A key feature of these separate procedures is that they are sporadic. When they began to be adopted, everyone understood that a modern population could not gather together regularly like the inhabitants of an ancient city, to decide the ordinary business of government. But a modern population could occasionally put its mind to the fundamental rules by which it was to be governed, without having to devote itself full-time to the details of politics. Accordingly, and inevitably, the rules acquired a certain permanence. When Jefferson in eighteenth-century America and Condorcet in eighteenth-century France proposed that constitutional legislation should automatically be revisited after twenty-five years, they were more or less in the target area; the American Constitution has been amended on average about once every twenty years since 1791, though there have been long periods when no alteration was made (twenty-six years since the last one, with no prospect of another in sight probably for a generation), and very few really fundamental alterations – maybe only four or five, depending on how one defines 'fundamental'.

The essence of the old British system was that this kind of semi-permanence was not built into legislation. In principle, the next Parliament could always undo the work of the previous one, and even if it baulked at doing so with important measures such as the extension of the franchise, it could certainly alter or adapt them, and not leave the business of working out their implications to a constitutional court. This was the well-known 'omnicompetence' of Parliament, obvious to everyone from the seventeenth century onwards, and true not just in constitutional matters: John Selden, a famous seventeenth-century jurist, observed that Parliament could make it a capital offence to stay in bed after eight o'clock, and Leslie Stephen 200 years later remarked that Parliament could legally order the death of all blue-eyed babies. One might have thought that this extraordinarily untrammelled power would be disastrous for civil liberties, but the central paradox of British constitutional history is that on the whole Britain has had a remarkable record for civil liberties, certainly as compared with most other long-established states. How has a legislature with absolute power coexisted with liberal political practices?

Some people might say that there is some special political culture in Britain that prevents Parliament from actually legislating for genocide, and that without this all hell would break loose; but this is a view rather too reminiscent of Kipling's contempt for 'Lesser Breeds without the Law'. I do not think there is some special magic in the island of Britain. I think that the omnicompetence of Parliament actually *bred* a culture of civil liberties, since no one faced permanent or semi-permanent defeat for their political projects. Every few years it was possible to reverse a measure, if necessary by forming some new coalition of interests to win the next general election; and if one lost, then it was through the relatively transparent force of the ballot box rather than the mysterious and apparently unfair power of a Supreme Court. This is one of the practical consequences of powerful democratic politics. Contrary to what people often suppose, democracy is actually a *means* to civil peace and toleration, and not in potential opposition to them. Bringing as many people as possible into the sphere of political decision-making, and allowing them as much freedom as possible to effect the outcome, calms political passion rather than inflaming it.

An obvious example of this is the difference between the UK and the US over abortion. In Britain, abortion was legalised by a straightforward Act of Parliament, and in principle it can be banned once more equally straightforwardly. The inability of anti-abortion activists to bring this about can then be ascribed purely to their ineffectiveness at persuading enough of their fellow citizens to support them. In the United States, on the other hand, it was legalised through a Supreme Court decision, something which it is extraordinarily difficult to overturn through a transparent political process. In Britain there is little hysterical opposition to the legislation; in the US people working in abortion clinics have routinely been murdered. This is exactly what one would expect if it is true that genuinely democratic processes tend to lower the level of anger in public life.

However, all this changed when Britain entered the EEC in 1973, though the working out of its implications took a long time, and the referendum campaign in 1975 as a consequence was much calmer than the campaign we have just experienced. Though the 1972 European Communities Act was an ordinary statute, it put in place a new kind of constitutional order in which fundamental rules governing British political, economic and social life could not be amended by the same process by which they had been enacted. It would be a mistake to say that Britain thereby 'lost its independence'; it is not clear how it could, and certainly the EU is not a superstate which has taken away national independence from its members. But the EU is a constitutional order for each member state, taken separately: it enacts fundamental rights and duties which the legislatures of the members cannot alter. The only way open to Parliament to change the rules is by a wholesale repudiation of the entire constitutional structure, in other words Brexit, and the same would be true in any other European state.

Harold Wilson's government duly recognised the gravity of this change when it introduced the first referendum in British history. Britain now had to have some supra-Parliamentary system for determining these fundamental rules since Parliament itself was no longer able to do so, and the Wilson government simply followed what had become the almost universal practice of modern states in turning to a constitutional plebiscite to provide the mechanism. The fact that referendums in Britain are notionally 'consultative' is irrelevant: no one seriously thinks that they should be ignored, any more than they seriously think that the Queen can veto a Parliamentary bill.

But the constitutional order represented by the EEC was exactly the sort of semi-permanent arrangement into which Britain had never previously locked itself, and the question of whether we should stay in the EU or not raised exactly the prospects of permanent victory or permanent defeat which had not formerly been on people's minds. Most Brexiteers understood that if the vote went against them, the issue would not be reopened for a generation or more; Remainers too paid lip service to this principle, though in the aftermath many have tried to pretend otherwise. We do not need to look anywhere else for an explanation of the hysteria and viciousness in public life during and after the campaign.

Exactly the same was true of the Scottish referendum campaign, which as I said was the first intimation of this aggressive and violent politics. Here too the idea of holding a referendum on Scottish independence made it a constitutional question of the modern kind, in which high passions were aroused. It should be said that the very action of giving Scotland the referendum actually gave the country its independence at the fundamental, constitutional level, since the Scottish people could now decide the basic terms of their common life (something the Spanish government has always understood in relation to Catalonia), and this was not significantly in debate – nobody denied the capacity of the Scots to make the decision. What made the campaign so vicious was that whatever conclusion the Scots came to in 2014 about what they wanted to do with this fundamental power was – or was believed to be – another decision which would be semi-permanent. The fact that both in Scotland and in Britain more widely the losing side is tempted to enter into what the Canadians have called a 'neverendum' does not alter the dynamic of this process, since the neverendum is always entirely one-sided. There was no question of quickly reopening the question if Independence had won in Scotland, or in Quebec, or if Remain had won in Britain. And as long as it is one-sided, the threat of permanent defeat for one side remains.

The key fact about what we have just lived through is that though one might think the two sides were on an equal footing in this regard, in that either Remain won permanently or Leave did so, it was the people who voted Remain who had wished to close down political possibilities much more than those who voted Leave. It was membership of the EU which limited the political space, and which over the years has induced a sense of powerlessness in the electorate, even if the root cause of this sense has not always been obvious. The vote for Brexit is an opportunity to cancel this: conservative politicians will still be able to argue for conservative measures, but socialist politicians can now argue for socialist ones, and they will have a fair fight in front of the voters. This would not have been true had we voted to remain; we have been handed the opportunity to return to our old politics, and we must not lose it.

17 May 2018

The morning after the referendum, like many people who had voted to Leave, I was in a mood to compromise. The result after all had been fairly close, and if a new constitutional settlement was to last, it had to compel quite widespread consent. I thought that membership of the EEA might be possible; certainly some kind of free-trade arrangement was imperative. Since June 2016, however, I have changed my mind, and I think I am not alone. The reason is partly that as I have thought more about the nature of the EEA and the role in it of the ECJ I have backed away from it as a solution; but the key reason is more profound than that. The behaviour of the leading supporters of remaining in the EU during the period after the referendum has made me deeply mistrustful of any compromise, since it is clear that all compromise proposals leave open a route quite quickly back into the EU in some fashion, and there are absolutely no grounds to think that the prominent Remainers will not seize the opportunity to go down it.

Trust has become the central issue in British politics. And in doing so, it has reminded us of one of the main objections to the EU, and explains why accusations of treason have alarmingly become a staple of the right-wing press in Britain. The EU is an institution which – despite all its window-dressing – is still essentially an *intergovernmental* organisation. Decisions are made through the familiar processes of international bargaining, though unlike other international bargains the ones made in the EU directly apply to the internal arrangements of the member states. And international negotiations have always been pre-eminently the arena in which governments act *secretly* and spring faits accomplis on their citizens. The age of the secret treaty may be over, though I wouldn't rule out the existence of a wide range of secret 'understandings' between modern states, particularly over such things as nuclear weapons. But secrecy in general is endemic in international relations. Because of this, even if a country's constitution gives the final say over an international agreement to the legislature (as ours arguably does not), in practice the negotiations are entirely in the hands of the executive, the repository of secrets in most modern states. International negotiations also tend to give a disproportionate role to the civil servants, the 'sherpas' in contemporary parlance, who prepare the ground for their (supposed) masters, since very few modern politicians have the time or the experience to pay as much attention to international politics as they do to the internal politics of their own countries. Their instincts are also likely to be much less acute when they leave the familiar territory in which they have made their careers.

This is the particularly toxic feature of the EU. A democratic state like the United Kingdom has, by and large, a pretty open debate about important domestic issues. There may be secret manoeuvrings within party executives and within Whitehall, but it all has to come out into the open before any firm decisions are made, and politicians can relatively easily be forced into U-turns. But to make important decisions through international bargaining, decisions which then structure the economy, and even to some extent the society, of a member state, as those made through the EU institutions must do, is to bring secrecy into the heart of domestic politics. With secrecy inevitably comes mistrust. As modern states do more and more through international agreements, distrust of politicians grows among their populations, who suspect that their ruling classes now have more in common with the ruling classes of other countries than they do with the ruled of their own. They may be right in this mistrust – after all, for much of the pre-democratic history of our countries this would have been an entirely well-founded apprehension – but even without a cultural sympathy of this kind the logic of the international structures makes a politician into a kind of secret agent within their own country. Who knows what they really want, and what they have implicitly as well as explicitly agreed to?

Defenders of the EU can agree with all this, and they can go on to say that for this reason it is vital to turn the EU into a proper state with the kind of transparent internal politics that we were used to in our individual nations fifty or sixty years ago. But as things stand that ambition looks absurdly utopian – far more utopian than anything Brexiteers are guilty of. Like so much of the EU, its political accountability is stuck in a half-way house, unable to move forward or backward. If we value transparency and trustworthiness in our politics, we have to leave the EU and detoxify our public life; until we have thoroughly disentangled ourselves from it, distrust will remain the default attitude of the British public, and nothing can be done about that during the interim period we have embarked upon. Remainers cannot avoid the distrust so many of us feel about them, and we would be extraordinarily foolish to suppose that they do not deserve it; in this respect, at least, there is a profound asymmetry between Leave and Remain, for no one seriously thinks that Leavers have a secret agenda – the whole point of their position is to throw open British politics once again to the public gaze, and public debate. There is – alas – no basis for compromise now between the sides.

15 July 2018:
How to Break Up the Union

A White Paper entitled 'The Future Relationship between the United Kingdom and the European Union', otherwise known as 'the Chequers plan', was agreed by the Cabinet at a meeting at Chequers on 6 July 2018. The Foreign Secretary, Boris Johnson, and the Secretary of State for Exiting the European Union, David Davis, both resigned in protest at the plan, on the grounds that it committed Britain to 'a common rulebook for all goods' with the EU, and to introduce a 'facilitated customs arrangement' which would function 'as if a combined customs territory' with the EU in order to 'ensure both sides meet their commitments to Northern Ireland and Ireland'.

Theresa May is fond of saying that her policy towards the EU is driven by her determination not to break up the Union – that is, the union between Britain and Northern Ireland. But there is another Union she seems to have forgotten about, and one which is much more important: the union between Scotland and England. Before the referendum, I argued that the drive for Scottish independence would be killed if the United Kingdom left the EU, since independence for Scotland inside an EU which also contained England was virtually costless, while independence (or even continued membership of the

EU for Scotland) if England was *not* in the EU imposed huge costs which the Scottish electorate would baulk at. Independence within the EU had been the strategy which propelled the SNP to its present position, once they had abandoned in the 1980s their old visceral hatred of the EEC, and the logic of the situation simply entailed that independence outside the EU would take the SNP back to where it started. Events after the referendum, I think, proved this prediction to be correct. Feeble bluster from the SNP leaders notwithstanding (and not all of them, at that), the steady trend was away from independence and back to something more like the old politics of Scotland inside the Union.

But the more the settlement with the EU looks like a kind of continued membership of the bloc, the more independence for Scotland will creep back onto the agenda. May is faced with an infernal balancing machine: to give the Ulster Unionists what they want, in the shape of no border down the Irish Sea, she runs the risk of erecting one on the Tweed. And to keep the possibility of a 'hard border' between England and Scotland at bay, she has to erect one in Ireland. Furthermore, a compromise of the sort she says she wants is radically unstable: to continue with the mechanical analogy, any slight perturbation in the future will tip the balance one way or another.

So what is to be done? If in fact there is a choice of this kind to be made, it is self-evident that it is the Union between Scotland and England which must be preserved. Indeed, if we were to believe what May says about her determination to preserve the United Kingdom, this consideration should override everything for her, including the convenience of Airbus.[38] But I am not sure that we have to make this choice. In the North of Ireland we have actually the same situation which the SNP planned to exploit: somewhere where questions of union or disunion are currently costless. Continued common membership of the EU for Britain and the Republic of Ireland would allow future Nationalists to argue that a united Ireland would have no real costs for Unionists, other than of a sentimental kind, and they would be right. They might not quickly win a majority, but nor did the SNP in their referendum on independence; eventually the underlying facts would assert themselves. I do not see that the logic in Ireland would be any different from that in Scotland, and it is worth remembering that Sinn Féin performed exactly the same volte-face as the SNP, going from their old hard-line opposition to a united Europe to their present posture of support for it – and they have seen their electoral fortunes rise in the same sort of way. But that means that the same logic applies to Ireland as to Scotland: the more we are in the EU, the more *breakup* rather than continued union is likely. It would not have been the present negotiations with the EU which would have forced a break, and that seems to be all May cares about; but if she were really to care about the actual possibility of the Union dissolving, the worst thing she could do would be to go down her present path.

1 August 2018

Negotiations between the UK and the EU over a Withdrawal Agreement continued during the summer without any very clear appearance of progress.

There is a general sense that the negotiations between Britain and the EU are a shambles, and that British politics in general is broken. This is clearly true in some ways, but we should not misunderstand what is happening, and fail to see that in part it is the welcome reawakening of long-dead political struggles. We tend to think that a single entity called 'Britain' entered another entity called 'Europe' and that what has mattered since is simply the relationship between these two entities. But in reality the EU and its predecessors – the Common Market and the EEC – were always used for internal British purposes, as a way of securing a semi-permanent victory for one side against its opponents. This process began right at the beginning: the Labour Party consistently opposed the various schemes for European unity in the 1950s, for reasons which Nye Bevan put very clearly in 1957: the Common Market, he said, represents 'the disenfranchisement of the people and the enfranchisement of market forces'. While Conservatives on the whole expressed enthusiasm for the Common Market precisely for the same reasons: they understood that its general character would make a return to full-blooded Attlee-style socialism almost impossible. It is no accident that Margaret Thatcher both voted for the European Communities Act and was an enthusiastic advocate of the Common Market's evolution into the single market we have today, with its extensive restrictions on state aid and its enforcement of a high degree of competition in European markets, including the labour market.

From the beginning they also welcomed the free movement of labour: the position paper presented to Macmillan's Cabinet in July 1960 which formed the basis of all the later negotiations with the EEC recognised that it would be the ultimate consequence of joining, but said, interestingly, that 'the movement of labour works both ways, and might conceivably be of advantage to us as a method of dealing with unemployment'[39] – not a sentiment we can imagine a Labour government ever expressing!

What the Conservatives who engineered Britain's membership of the EEC were not keen on, on the other hand, was the protectionist tariff regime. The same position paper went so far as to state about temperate foodstuffs that:

> It seems out of the question that we could accept the common tariff or the other protective devices ... for these products ... because of the impact on the Commonwealth, the damage to our trading relations with third countries – in the case of the United States a breakdown of the Trade Agreement – and the consequences for food prices here.[40]

The UK had had a trade agreement with the US since 1938, but it was terminated in 1962 on the grounds that it was largely redundant given GATT. But the timing of its termination is suggestive, given that it was in the middle of the first negotiations to join the EEC. In 1960 the Cabinet had not supposed that the agreement with the US was redundant, despite the fact that a couple of months earlier the EEC had lowered its common external tariff to fit in with GATT and membership of the EEC should therefore (on the reasoning of two years later) not have conflicted with the US agreement.

Both political parties in Britain had traditionally had an ambiguous relationship to protectionism, with Baldwin's government in the 1930s introducing a range of restrictions on free trade at the same time as many members of the Labour Party opposed them. By the 1950s free trade was once more the ideal on both sides of the spectrum, but it is fair to say that on the whole in the post-war period Labour's instincts were more protectionist than the Conservatives', something which became very clear with the so-called Alternative Economic Strategy of the 1970s and 1980s, which attracted a great deal of support from within the party, and which the present leader of the party still seems to espouse in large part. Labour's hostility to the Common Market was rarely based on a commitment to general free trade; instead, for some people, such as Richard Crossman, their vision for Britain was that it should be what he proudly described as 'a socialist offshore island', while for others (notably Hugh Gaitskell in his famous speech to the party conference in 1962) it was as a continued part of a Commonwealth trading area with, to a degree, a common external tariff.

We should not, incidentally, underestimate the importance of the Commonwealth to Labour thinking, or treat it as the imperial anachronism it may have been for the Conservatives. Denis Healey in his pamphlet against the Coal and Steel Community in 1950 proclaimed that 'by transforming four hundred millions of Britain's Asian subjects into friends and equal partners the Labour Government has built a bridge between East and West, between the white and coloured peoples', and this sense of the Commonwealth as an alternative to the wholly European – and white – schemes for unity was widely felt on the Left in the 1950s and 1960s. But the critical point is that whatever the actual area which had protective tariffs against the rest of the world, whether Britain by itself or the Commonwealth, on the whole members of the Labour Party felt comfortable with the principle of protectionism.

Once Britain entered the EEC, each party had something it wanted. For the Conservatives it offered a means of entrenching a market economy, while for the Labour Party it offered an alternative to a world of unrestrained global free trade. But the benefit to the Conservatives was incomparably greater, since for them accepting the level of protectionism which the EEC provided was a small price to pay compared with the epochal advantage of – in effect – constitutionalising a market-based economy and society. A few gestures to workers' rights by the EEC in the 1980s won over some more Labour members, but compared (for example) to the steady encroachment on the real power of trades unions across the Continent under the aegis of the ECJ, these gestures were pretty hollow. But now, as the prospect of Brexit looms, British politics has reverted to the contestation which had been frozen for forty years.

For many Conservative opponents of the EU, the great prize that is within reach is what they always wanted: entrenchment of a market at the domestic level, and full freedom internationally to participate in a global market. For these people, entrenchment of the market could be achieved through something like the Chequers proposals, but it could also be achieved through continued membership of the EEA, since the EEA is in effect a subsidiary of the EU's single market, but is outside the customs union. It is no accident that Daniel Hannan for a long time has advocated the EEA route, and the prospect may be gathering momentum in right-wing circles. Labour's instinct, on the other hand, is to stay in 'a' customs union with the EU – not necessarily because the leaders of the party actually want this in its own right, since some of them are clearly genuine Brexiteers, but because if some kind of compromise has to be engineered they are not as unhappy with a customs union as they would be with continued membership of the single market.

Given this history, it is not surprising that British politics now appears to be in a condition of crisis, since the original temptation which was put in front of post-war politicians, that they could lock in their own policies for their country in near perpetuity, is still there, even if full membership of the EU is no longer (we presume) available to them. They are playing for high stakes, and we should not expect them to do so in an atmosphere of calm. Labour's position in this struggle, however, is not quite the same as the Conservatives', since for many Remainers in the party (I think) the EU is not *intrinsically* desirable. What they want is to stop the Conservatives using a post-EU settlement to achieve the domestic goals the Conservatives always wanted – this is why, despite the manifest evidence to the contrary, so many people on the Left cling to the idea that outside the EU workers' rights in Britain would be undermined. What they have instinctively spotted is that some versions of a Britain outside the EU might indeed lock in a Thatcherite economy, though what they fail to see is that a Britain inside the EU would fare little better.

But if this is right, the best prospect the Left has for defeating this possibility is the hardest Brexit that can be contrived. A customs union nowadays will not remain as merely an old-fashioned common external tariff system; it will increasingly be configured through the judgments of the ECJ (which will have to be involved in some fashion) into a system with considerable domestic reach, which will inevitably be of a neoliberal character, given the fundamentally market-based structures of the EU. The only thing which will allow the Left to roll back the last forty years of market entrenchment is opening up a space in which democratic politics can determine the shape of the British economy, and British society in general, as it did from the coming of universal suffrage until 1 January 1973. If at some point the electorate votes for Conservative policies, so be it; the policies can at least be reversed through the simple means of a general election, rather than what we are finding to be the agonising process of breaking away from a supranational entity.

These are big issues, of an extremely far-reaching kind, and one would not expect a democratic society to be in anything other than turmoil about them. The key thing is for us all to recognise this, and not lose our nerve: the turmoil itself does not matter, and is indeed the outward sign of a healthy politics, just as the dramatic moments recently in the House of Commons are the outward sign of its waking to its old role after its forty-year sleep. What *would* matter would be a desire to suppress the turmoil by forcing us back into the structures of the EU, whether actually under that name or not. If the politics of the last couple of generations is broken, so much the better, and we must live with that fact until democracy has properly re-established itself.

19 November 2018:
The Surprising Benefits to
Ireland of a No-Deal Brexit

On 14 November 2018 the 'Draft Agreement on the Withdrawal of the United Kingdom from the European Union' was published. The agreement itself was mostly concerned with transitional arrangements such as the status of EU and UK citizens in the others' jurisdictions, continuity for bank accounts, etc. But it also contained a protocol detailing what came to be known as 'the Irish backstop', in which the UK expressed its commitment 'to protect North–South cooperation and its guarantee of avoiding a hard border, including any physical infrastructure or related checks and controls, and bearing in mind that any future arrangements must be compatible with these overarching requirements', and in order to secure this it agreed to create a 'single customs territory between the Union and the United Kingdom'. Professor David Grewal of Yale Law School and I published the following article in the Irish Times.

It is taken for granted on both sides of the Irish Sea that the worst kind of Brexit, from the point of view of the relationship between the United Kingdom and the Republic, is one in which Britain 'crashes out' of the EU without a negotiated settlement. The Northern Ireland Secretary has even said recently that if Britain trades with the EU under WTO rules there will have to be a hard border in Ireland, and that this may undermine the Common Travel Agreement between the two countries. But surprisingly, 'no deal' may in fact be the *best* kind of Brexit for the two countries.

To understand this, we first have to remember that Britain and the Republic already offer one another's citizens privileges which other EU citizens do not enjoy. There is in effect a passport union between the UK and Ireland, with freedom of movement for British and Irish citizens, no restrictions on employment, and immediate rights to vote in Parliamentary as well as local elections. This is the case without there being any need to check at the border whether anyone crossing it is a British or Irish citizen. So an obvious question is, in the event of a 'no-deal' Brexit, why could goods not be treated in the same way as people, with goods crossing the land border in Ireland being privileged and treated differently from those coming from elsewhere in the EU?

The immediate answer to this question is that WTO rules would preclude it. They do not permit one member to allow special trading privileges to a province of another member, and for these purposes the EU counts as a single country, being a customs union with its own membership of the WTO. So if a Britain outside the EU wished to grant the same kind of privileges to Irish goods that it does to Irish people, it would clearly fall foul of the WTO. All it could do would be to allow free trade for all EU goods, and under the WTO rules it would then have to do the same for all other members of the WTO. Though some people in Britain have advocated precisely this, it is politically difficult and may be undesirable.

But there are some exceptions to the scope of the WTO rules. Among them, Article XXI of the GATT, which governs the WTO, states, 'Nothing in this Agreement shall be construed ... to prevent any contracting party from taking any action which it considers necessary for the protection of its essential security interests ... taken in time of war or other emergency in international relations' (XXI.b.3). This is the clause which Trump has been using to introduce aggressive tariffs against a variety of countries, though without a shred of justification, at least in the case of Canada! But Britain can use the same clause in a perfectly justifiable manner, and *lower* tariffs in the name of security rather than raise them.

The clause has in fact quite frequently been invoked in trade disputes, and there is now a lot of case law, of a somewhat vague kind, about it. But almost all the disagreements over whether it can legitimately be invoked have been about whether it is (to use the technical term) 'self-justifying' – that is, whether a country can unilaterally declare a security risk and activate the Article. But this is not relevant to the Irish border question, since all the governments concerned have already agreed that an open border is required for security purposes – the Joint Report of December 2017 which introduced the idea of the Irish backstop, after all, begins the relevant section with the declaration that 'Both Parties affirm that the achievements, benefits and commitments of the peace process will remain of paramount importance to peace, stability and reconciliation', and politicians on all sides referred at the time to the danger of renewed violence if a hard border reappeared. So much so, in fact, that right-wing figures in Britain talked about being blackmailed by the gunmen!

If the argument about the risk to security in Ireland is to be taken seriously, then Britain can at least mount a case before the WTO that privileging goods from the Republic is justified, and open the border while the issue is being decided and while (one can suppose) proper negotiations are conducted with the EU. It should be said that it is only opening the *land* border in this way which could be justified under Article XXI; goods shipped from the Republic directly to the island of Britain would come under whatever tariff regime Britain put in place against the EU as a whole. But it is the land border which has been the focus of attention in the negotiations between the UK and the EU, and which has threatened to abort the whole process.

What would be the practical implications of unilaterally opening up the Irish border under Article XXI? One consequence would obviously be that some EU trade with the UK which currently comes via (say) Rotterdam would switch to being shipped to the UK via Ireland – which would be of benefit to both the Republic and Northern Ireland. It is unlikely, however, that enormous volumes of trade would be switched in the near future, as tariffs under the WTO (as many people have observed) are not particularly onerous, and the extra cost and trouble of switching to an Irish land route into the UK would probably not be worth it for most shippers. The vast majority of goods crossing the border would be likely still to originate in Ireland, and they are precisely the goods which under this kind of arrangement the UK would want to privilege.

If this state of affairs were to persist for some time, new businesses might want to open in the Republic in preference to the rest of the EU, and that would be even more to the interests of the Republic; the entire island of Ireland would in effect have been turned into a free port, along the lines of the suggestion made some months ago in the *Irish Times* by Professor Philip Pettit of Princeton, though he envisaged a formal agreement rather than unilateral action by Britain. Eventually this arrangement would probably be superseded by some more satisfactory deal with the EU than any of those currently on offer, but in the meantime the Republic would have possessed a useful bargaining counter in its own dealings with the EU, for example on corporation tax. The Taoiseach has said it is important that any measures the UK takes concerning the border should not be easy for it to reverse, and this is a very reasonable demand; but unilateral opening under Article XXI could not straightforwardly be reversed under WTO rules unless it was agreed that there were no longer security implications in having an open border.

How might the EU respond to a move of this kind by the UK? It too is now committed to keeping an open border in Ireland for security reasons. Could it restrict traffic from the North into the South if the UK was not restricting traffic in the opposite direction? And even if it tried, would the Irish government put up with this for a moment? It is very hard to imagine. Since the EU certainly cannot introduce a trade frontier between the Republic and the rest of the Union, it would be hoist on its own petard, and might come bitterly to regret introducing the issue of Irish security.[41]

16 January 2019

On 15 January 2019 the House of Commons rejected the Withdrawal Agreement by a vote of 432 to 202, though the vote did not require the government to abandon the Agreement.

Although the punditocracy are almost united in declaring May's Withdrawal Agreement dead, at least in its present form, as so often in the past they may all be wrong. The most important question in British politics is now the following. Suppose May allows the clock to run down towards 29 March, through a choreographed set of 'talks' both with opposition members and with the EU which are intentionally designed on her part to produce no changes in the Agreement. What will the various factions in Parliament do on (let us say) 27 March? We know what the genuine Brexiteers will do, viz., nothing. But what will Tory Remainers and Labour Remainers do? They will no doubt express fury and insist that Article 50 is postponed. But under the terms of the Article itself that cannot happen unless the government agrees, and on a matter as important as this it is hard to see any way in which a resolute government could be made to follow the will of the Commons, as long as it is still in power. Moreover exit day is defined as 29 March 2019 in the European Union

(Withdrawal) Act of 2018, and that will be very hard to alter without government support. So the Remainers face their worst nightmare: no deal on 29 March. Tory Remainers' nerves are likely to crack at this point. But that is not enough to give May her victory if Labour Remainers continue to oppose the Agreement. So the key issues are, first, what would Corbyn do in this situation, and, second, would the whole of his party support him? My own conjecture is that Corbyn himself would not be sorry to see no deal on 29 March, particularly if the consequent recrimination wrecked the Tory Party. But would his Remainers go along with this? It is hard to believe. Either they would rebel in sufficiently large numbers to pass the Agreement, or they would force Corbyn to change tack. So, paradoxically, May's defeat yesterday is a major threat to the unity of the Labour Party, even more than to the unity of the Tories. Her strategy, I believe, is plain: to run the clock down and peel off enough Labour Remainers to ensure the passage of her Agreement, if possible in precisely its present form. And judging by the attitudes of the Labour Remainers, this is a strategy which is, unfortunately, likely to succeed.

17 January 2019:
Deal or No Deal

A simple question: are we in a better position to make a deal with the EU after leaving it, or before? The persistent refrain that we are faced with a choice between May's Deal and No Deal is entirely misleading. The choice is in fact between a deal now and a deal later, as no one seriously thinks that there will not eventually be *some* kind of trade arrangement with the EU. So the choice is better phrased not as Deal or No Deal, but as Deal Now or Deal Later. While in theory May's agreement is itself supposed to be superseded by a later one, most people concerned seem effectively to have given up the pretence that if it is ratified there will ever be a significantly different later settlement, so our choice is indeed Now or Later.

There is an equally simple answer to the question. There is every reason for the EU to offer a very bad deal before we leave, in the hope that as a consequence we may not leave at all. Only if we have clearly and decisively left will we be able to make any kind of beneficial arrangement for the future. Moreover, even May herself might prefer it: her instinct, as many people have observed, seems to be to kick every can in sight down the road for as long as possible, and Deal Later allows her to do this much more effectively than Deal Now. Is there anything we might want which could only be achieved before we leave, rather than afterwards? Not even the terms of the existing Withdrawal Agreement, we can presume; if they were offered as the basis of a future relationship, why would the EU refuse them, given that they have accepted them before exit? But equally, we might not want to make the offer, once we had had time to consider the issues involved without the intense time pressure we are currently under. Deal Later gives everyone involved in this sorry spectacle breathing space; and given the enormous importance of the issues involved, and the danger of making a wrong choice which will govern our affairs for another generation, even a degree of disruption to some of our overseas trade is a price worth paying – and it is quite likely that the disruption will be less than is currently feared. We should not be bounced by a combination of the short-termism of restless capital and the short-termism of politicians into making important decisions in a panic.

23 January 2019

The British press at the moment is full of anxiety about whether, under the various Brexit schemes that are washing around, the UK will be a 'rule taker' from the EU without having any say in the making of the rules. But what is largely overlooked is that in many ways *all* the member states of the EU are to a great extent rule takers, with little or no say over the making of the rules. This is not because of the so-called 'democratic deficit' that supporters of the EU have long decried, and have hoped to alleviate by boosting the powers of the European Parliament, but because the governing principles of the EU are enshrined in treaties which cannot in any practical circumstances be reworked, and whose interpretation is in the hands of a court over which there cannot be proper political control.

There has now been extensive debate on the Left of British politics over whether a Labour Party programme of the kind outlined in the last manifesto could in fact be implemented within the EU. Since the debate turns on the question of what the famous 'four freedoms' enshrined in the EU treaties actually imply – for example, what kind of state aid is possible – the argument is in reality entirely about what the judgment of the ECJ might be, and not about what is theoretically feasible. Everything would depend on how good the lawyers in front of the court were, and what the judges felt like on that day. And unlike in the UK, there is no legislative or political mechanism available to any of the member states of the EU, even acting in concert, to overturn a judgment of their court, without rewriting the treaties.

Americans have long been familiar with this problem, and with the passions it arouses: the notorious Citizens United judgment, which undermined the more or less settled law over campaign finance, is a clear instance, and no doubt many more such judgments lie in wait down the road now Trump is changing the composition of the court. But at least in America, as we have recently seen, there is *some*, albeit fallible, political process which can affect the judgments of the court, and there is even a means to amend the Constitution which does not require unanimity among all the states of the Union. Neither of these two things apply in the case of the EU. There is a further point which Dr Gunnar Beck, an expert on the ECJ, has repeatedly stressed: the ECJ is not formally as bound by its own earlier decisions as are both the US and the UK Supreme Courts, making the business of second-guessing its determinations even more hazardous.

A future Labour manifesto, if the Remainers in the party get their way, will have to read something like the following: 'If elected, we are committed to introducing state aid to industries in deprived areas outside London in order to redress the damage done by years of free-market policies, as long as we can find some first-rate lawyers who can persuade a court over which we have no power to see the justice of our arguments, and failing that we are committed to abandoning our policies.' That at least would be honest, though it is hard to see it exciting the electorate – and there in a nutshell you have the problem with membership of the EU.

24 February 2019

On 15 January 2019, five days of debate in the Commons on the Withdrawal Agreement ended with a 'Meaningful Vote' in which the government suffered a huge defeat, losing by 230 votes. The following day Theresa May won a vote of confidence, but during the next four weeks she repeatedly failed to get the Commons to back her Withdrawal Agreement, and various alternative approaches were also outvoted.

Let us be clear about the reason for the humiliating shambles in which the British government, and Britain itself, currently find themselves. It is entirely straight-forward: once the serious possibility of a second referendum was raised by the EU's supporters within Britain, the EU had no incentive whatsoever to agree to any reasonable deal. The perfect outcome from the EU's perspective would be for a second referendum to annul the result of the first, and as we all know the EU is practised in using this technique on recalcitrant members. But the best way of securing a second referendum would be to make the process of leaving so complex and difficult that no one could seriously support whatever deal emerged from it. In an article for the *Daily Telegraph* on 15 November last year Tony Blair gave the game away:

The people need to tell us: in the light of all we now know, and two years of hideously complex and tangled negotiation, what do you want to do? Do you want to go forward with Brexit? In which case it is true Brexit you will get with a Prime Minister who believes in it. Or do you want to stay in Europe, and I would hope with a new European offer to the British people. Both sides would accept the outcome is final at least for a generation. I for one, if we vote again for Brexit, would get behind it and do everything I could to make a success of a new future for Britain.

The natural question to put to Blair is, if you would accept the result of a second referendum, why not accept the result of the first? And his only answer is, we did not know in 2016 what we know now. But what we 'know' has been *created* by the EU in the hope that we will be driven by it into another referendum. The 'facts' are actually *artefacts*. Ask yourself what would have happened if Blair and people like him had said on the morning of 24 June 2016, 'I for one will get behind Brexit and do everything I can to make a success of a new future.' What would the EU have done? Would it still have made the process of leaving so impossible, if it had believed the referendum result was irreversible 'for a generation'? And if it had not done so, what we 'know' now would have been quite different.

But as Blair also said in this article, 'we are where we are'. How should we go forward? The first thing to say is that to countenance a second referendum in the near future is simply to fall for the trick which has been played on us. I say this as someone who is a believer in referendums on constitutional matters (which is after all the norm in most modern states); but a second referendum in the near future would patently be a corruption of a democratic process. Suppose that it had been proposed beforehand that there should be two referendums on EU membership, one in June 2016 and the other in June 2019, and that the second one would be binding for twenty-five years or so, the usual breathing space between major constitutional decisions. Such a suggestion would surely have been laughed out of court. And if by some collective fit of idiocy the proposal had been adopted, no one would have taken the first referendum seriously, since they would have reserved all their arguments for a debate before the second and authoritative one. Similarly, one can presume, the EU would not have entered into any serious negotiation about the shape of relations between itself and an independent UK before the result of the final referendum was known: why should it have offered any concessions which might have encouraged people to vote for independence in the belief that the future relationship between the UK and the EU would be fine? Only presented with a clear and effectively permanent fait accompli would the EU have been willing to enter into proper discussions about the future. But if this is what would have been thought ahead of time, it is cheating the voters in the first referendum now to say that their decision was after all not final.

The second thing to say is that if the campaign for the so-called 'People's Vote' (the name, incidentally, a masterstroke of marketing) does succeed, it is imperative that the referendum does not include staying in the EU (or 're-joining') as an option. Constitutional decisions, as I have said, should not be treated in this frivolous fashion, constantly reopened until one side can unilaterally declare the matter fixed for a generation, and in the case of membership of the EU, bind the country into arrangements which it will be increasingly difficult ever to leave. For this last reason, it is important to observe, Leave and Remain are not in fact symmetrical positions. Leave offers nothing that can't relatively easily be altered any time in the future, while Remain offers the opposite – that fact, after all, is precisely why it is possible for the Remainers to call for a second referendum on membership.

Trade arrangements without major constitutional implications, on the other hand, have always been decided through normal Parliamentary processes. But if enough people feel strongly that there ought to be plebiscites on them, there is no particular reason to resist – though the same logic would extend plebiscites into many other areas of governmental action, something (one assumes) the Blairite Remainers would baulk at. One suspects, however, that the last thing they really want is a 'People's Vote' covering only the terms of Brexit, and not its principle, since that would certainly entrench the break between Britain and the EU for a generation.

12 April 2019:
Modest Proposals

After the Withdrawal Agreement was again defeated on 12 March, the government began the process of asking for an extension of the Article 50 period. The initial request was for an extension until 30 June; the European Council offered an extension until 22 May if the Withdrawal Agreement was passed by 29 March, the original end of the Article 50 period. On 29 March, with pro-Brexit demonstrations on Parliament Square, the Agreement was again defeated. May asked for another extension until 30 June, but the European Council on 10 April gave an extension until 31 October, on condition that the UK held European Parliamentary elections in May.

In a few years, Britain is supposed to have a general election. Unfortunately, it is already clear that there is a serious possibility that a government might be elected whose policies would do serious damage to the British economy. Expert economists both inside and outside the Treasury assure us that the kind of left-wing programme which the current Labour Party might implement could significantly reduce our GDP for some years, and almost irretrievably damage our relationships with our leading trade and security partners around the world. Fortunately, at the moment we have in the House of Commons a body of MPs who have shown that they grasp the dangers of these kinds of developments, and have been willing to stand up for what they believe to be the good of their country. It would be extremely foolish at this point in our history to risk the prospect of this well-informed and patriotic group of MPs being replaced by a much more radical crowd who might undo all the good work our current MPs have done, such as making sure that the United Kingdom stayed in the EU.

Accordingly, I propose that Parliament should now vote for an extension to the life of the present Parliament. Such an extension might need to be no more than a few months, in the course of which popular enthusiasm for a left-wing party might have diminished sufficiently for there to be little risk in holding an election; but if Parliament were to judge that the danger remained, further extensions would be in order until our economic well-being was secured and our accustomed international role was wholly safe. Some people might say that such a thing would be unprecedented, and would fly in the face of democracy; but they may have forgotten that the greatest of all English Parliaments, the Long Parliament of 1640, did precisely this, and sat without a new general election until 1653, despite being legally obliged to hold an election every three years. It is true that dissident minorities such as the Levellers protested at this, but it was precisely to keep such people (and supporters of the monarch) from ruining their country that the members of the Long Parliament acted as they did. Since we now understand that it is not the mere fact that they have been elected, but the much more important fact that they possess special insight into the needs of their country, which has given the MPs their authority, surely no one could object to a few extensions until democracy no longer threatens our economy.

There is another and less radical alternative. As both the Chancellor of the Exchequer and the leader of the Labour Party have correctly observed, people do not vote to be poorer. Accordingly, after the election a body of peer-reviewed experts could determine whether or not the policy of an incoming left-wing government would damage the economy. If they concluded that it would, the election result could simply be set aside on the grounds that it did not in fact represent the will of the British people, and the losing party could be declared the winner, with an appropriate adjustment of their seats in Parliament. Unlike the other proposal, this would have the merit of providing an intake to the Commons of new members, without threatening the fundamentals of our economic and foreign policies.

(Friends have pointed out that it may be necessary in the current political climate to emphasise that these proposals are what once was understood as 'satire'. The fact that they might be read wholly seriously, and that heads would nod in agreement, tells one all one needs to know about our strange times.)

3 June 2019

On 24 May Theresa May announced that she proposed to resign as leader of the Conservative Party, her resignation taking effect on 7 June. She would continue as Prime Minister until a new leader of the party was chosen, at the latest by 24 July, and was able to take office.

In an interview with Michal Matlak in the *New York Review of Books Daily* for 29 May, Michel Barnier dropped a remark which was widely reported – and indeed gave the *NYR* the title for its piece. He explained the Brexit vote by 'typically British reasons: the hope for a return to a powerful global Britain, nostalgia for the past – nostalgia serves no purpose in politics'. This is a particularly revealing remark, as it captures the persistent misunderstanding on the Continent about Brexit, and indeed about British history, and it explains a lot about the inability of Barnier and his companions to understand the politics of Brexit.

Historians argue about the extent to which the British Empire was ever very popular among a large part of the British population, but there is no doubt that for much of the nineteenth and early twentieth centuries it was far from enthusiastically supported by the British working classes. The description of the Empire by the Chartists captured what many of the working-class population thought of it: for them, as they struggled for democracy and labour rights at home, the Empire was 'the outworks of the citadel of corruption', bolstering the power of the domestic ruling class. Many people on the Left (including Engels) believed that immigration from the Empire had driven British wages down – immigration, that is, from Ireland – and the profits of empire were extremely unequally distributed across the British population. The imperial possessions which later became the Dominions obviously offered many opportunities for members of the working class to make a better life, but the fact that they were governed by the British Crown was largely irrelevant: the United States, outside the Empire, always remained the most popular destination for emigrants. The Empire was the most striking fact about Britain in the eyes of foreign observers, but it was not the object of loyalty and enthusiasm *within* Britain which they supposed it to be.

Accordingly, we are not going to find much nostalgia for the Empire among the working-class communities which voted to leave the EU. If there is any nostalgia there, I suspect it is nostalgia for the years between 1940 and 1951 when the Labour Party was in government and was able to put into place what increasingly in retrospect has come to seem a remarkably radical set of policies, against a background of a high degree of common purpose. The deep commitment to the NHS, and the sense (evinced by the ceremonies opening the London Olympics) that it may be the only reliable index of a British identity, is a major legacy of those years, and testimony to their power in the popular imagination. Not coincidentally, it was the Attlee government which made the first and decisive move in the dismantling of the Empire.

It is not clear that the right-wing politicians who support Brexit are nostalgic for the Empire, either. Again, if there is nostalgia there, it is for a much older, pre-imperial Britain, before its trading relationships had fossilised into direct rule over colonised populations. That certainly seems to be true of the more thoughtful of them, such as Daniel Hannan, whose imagination in fact seems most to be captivated by the England of Shakespeare's day, long before Britain was a 'global' power (or indeed Britain existed as a political entity). The stress these people put on relatively small countries such as Singapore engaging in global free trade does not look very much like a hankering after the Empire.

The deep irony in what Barnier said is that if one were to look for the group in the UK who most long for something like the British Empire, one would find it in the supporters and not the opponents of the EU. This goes right back to the beginning of the movement to bring Britain into the European Communities, when the Macmillan and Heath governments constantly emphasised the need to enter the Communities in order to (as Macmillan's Cabinet was told) prevent 'the risk of losing political influence and of ceasing to be able to exercise any claim to be a World Power'.[42] Even under Harold Wilson, to the alarm of Richard Crossman, the chief argument presented by the Foreign Office for continuing to apply for membership was (of all things) to preserve both Britain's role East of Suez and the sterling area. Economic considerations played a remarkably small part in these discussions during the 1960s and 1970s: keeping up Britain's post-imperial presence was the dominating theme.

The kind of person who is particularly keen on the European 'project' is still the kind of person who in their grandfathers' or (now) great-grandfathers' day would have been happy running the Empire, while telling themselves that it was really a force for liberal political values. We are used to thinking about the EU as a product of the Second World War in Europe, and as (supposedly) a means of keeping the peace on the Continent; but we should not forget that it also came into existence in precisely the years in which the European colonial empires were being dismantled. The EU offered itself as a kind of alternative stage upon which these old imperial ruling classes could regain something of the role they had lost, making lives (as they thought) better for populations who had no direct say in how they were being governed. This is the 'nostalgia' that underpinned and still underpins the EU, while the 'nostalgia' of Brexit is in reality a desire for a final emancipation from the burden of empire.

5 July 2019

From late May onwards influential voices in the Labour Party became increasingly strident in support of a policy of 'Remain and Reform'; a good example would be an article by Paul Mason in The Guardian *on 27 May entitled 'Corbynism is now in crisis: the only way forward is to oppose Brexit'.*

'Tough on crime, tough on the causes of crime.' 'Remain and Reform.' Tony Blair and his admirers have never been at a loss when it comes to fine-sounding but deeply dishonest slogans. As we all know now, Blair's government was far tougher on crime than on the causes of crime, with the prison population going from 60,000 to 80,000 during his time in office and little to show for it in terms of the reduction in crime. Whatever 'tough on the causes of crime' may have meant, in practice Blair's policy turned out to be little more than a standard regime of increased policing and incarceration. It was really just 'tough on crime', and the underlying causes were never seriously addressed, in part because no one really knew what they might be.

Exactly the same is going to be true of 'Remain and Reform', if by some evil chance it ever comes to be implemented. This is the new slogan for Labour Remainers, inspired by Yanis Varoufakis, for whom it has been the solution to his own personal dilemma – the contradiction between his experience in the Greek debt crisis and his long-standing romance with the idea of a united Europe. It is actually testimony to the truth of what those of us on the Left who have supported Brexit have said all along, that as things stand in the EU many socialist policies are impossible – can there really be traditional socialism in a Union governed by the four freedoms? If this is not the case, what is the need for 'Reform'?

The argument for 'Remain', for many of the people who support 'Remain and Reform', is that we need to stay in the EU in order to stop a Tory government implementing a programme that will undermine workers' rights and make Britain a capitalist offshore island. But the idea that the EU is needed to stop such a thing presupposes that domestic British political processes will not do so in any reliable fashion – otherwise we could simply rely on the force of Labour's arguments delivering it victories at the ballot box. So underlying the 'Remain and Reform' agenda is a pessimism about British politics, and a belief that it will not deliver the kind of results the Left hopes for. But if we despair of British politics, why should we expect anything better from the politics of Europe? Anyone looking at the Continent today with clear eyes and a clear head is not going to think that the Left is poised to take it over – if anything, the complete opposite is true. So where is 'Reform' going to come from? There is a contradiction at the heart of 'Remain and Reform' just as there was at the heart of 'Tough on crime, tough on the causes of crime.'

Not only are the appropriate political formations lacking across Europe, it is not clear what the appropriate processes would be. Essentially, the EU is a legal order, with its most important decisions made by a court interpreting a constitution – as the Lisbon Treaty should have been called. In this respect it resembles the United States, though since it was created to entrench a certain kind of market society and not to fashion a state, its constitution arguably has further-reaching economic implications than even the US Constitution. But the Left in the United States, and indeed the general American population, has always understood the significance of this structure and is properly informed about it. Political scientists produce detailed studies of how the Supreme Court operates and how the social and political background of the justices affects the result; Presidential elections increasingly focus on who Presidents will nominate and who can get through the Senate confirmation. Activists dream of constitutional amendments, such as one overturning the notorious Citizens United judgment, and they even have more or less practical plans to secure them – or at least they know what is required. How many members of the Labour Party calling for 'Remain and Reform' can even name one of the judges of the ECJ, let alone how they might rule on a case, or how the provisions of the treaties which they are interpreting could be changed?

For example, at the moment, Article 153 (5) of the Consolidated Treaty expressly excludes from the competence of the EU anything to do with 'pay, the right of association, the right to strike or the right to impose lock-outs', all things which you would expect the Left to be interested in. How could that be changed? (Hint: if the powers of the union are to be extended, the European Council has to agree to put any proposed amendment to a special convention 'composed of representatives of the national Parliaments, of the Heads of State or Government of the Member States, of the European Parliament and of the Commission', which has to 'adopt by consensus a recommendation to a conference of representatives of the governments of the Member States', each of which has then separately to ratify the proposed amendment before it can come into force. If there are any hold-outs, 'the matter shall be referred to the European Council' – who will be really, really angry? Or what?)

Contrast these procedures with Article V of the US Constitution, dealing with amendments, which gives no

veto power to any governmental institutions such as
the presidency or the state governors, and even allows
two-thirds of the state legislatures to force a constitutional convention on an unwilling Congress; and no one
thinks it is an easy matter to amend the US Constitution
in a progressive (or, indeed, any) direction. Can anyone
seriously think that there is any route to 'Reform' in the
EU, without what is at the moment an unimaginable transformation of the domestic politics in every single member
state? And if there were to be such a transformation,
would there be any need for the EU? Wouldn't these
left-wing democratic states manage relationships between
themselves without the need for supranational regulation
and technocratic government?

So, just as 'Tough on crime, tough on the causes of
crime' really meant simply 'Tough on crime', 'Remain and
Reform' really means 'Remain' – or maybe 'Remain but
let's keep our fingers crossed that it might change.' The
people who mouth this slogan have to come clean with the
rest of us: would they support Remain without Reform, or
is Reform a necessary condition for Remain? In almost all
cases, I think, it is the former. But they then have to say
openly that the kind of things they mean by 'Reform', and
which used to be thought of as 'Socialism', are expendable
in the interests of staying in the EU, and they have to tell
us why they are willing to make that trade-off, rather than
pretending that it does not have to be made.

18 July 2019

After discussion at Westminster and in the press about whether a new Prime Minister could prorogue Parliament in order to prevent it from halting a no-deal Brexit on 31 October, an amendment tacked onto the Northern Ireland (Executive Formation) Bill, intended to prevent prorogation between 9 October and 18 December, was passed by a majority of forty-one. Four Cabinet members, including the Chancellor, abstained.

All sorts of constitutional arguments which at the mid-twentieth century seemed to have been settled have reawakened under the stress of Britain's membership of the EU. What we have been living through is one of the great periods of constitutional upheaval which have marked British history every hundred years or so, and when the dust settles we shall be looking out over a new landscape – though in some respects it is a landscape which would have been familiar to Englishmen 300 years ago. In particular, we have been forced to think hard about what 'sovereignty' means, and where it is located in the British system.

Until recently, the answer would have been 'in Parliament' or, if one was being ultra-precise, 'in the Queen in Parliament', and this answer is still given today

by a faction within the British establishment which wants
to use Parliament to control Brexit (though they usually
mean by Parliament the two Houses, or perhaps only the
Commons, and not the Crown or the Crown's ministers).
But this was only ever true in a limited sense. Only laws
made with the consent of Queen, Lords and Commons
have ultimate legal validity, though there have always
been very general statutes which granted a high degree of
effective law-making to other entities, notably ministers of
the Crown and (since 1973) functionaries of the EU. But
if one goes beyond this legal doctrine and asks 'Why does
this group of people meeting in a rather shabby building
on the banks of the Thames possess sovereignty?', the
realistic answer for many hundreds of years has been that
they represent the British people as a whole, and that the
ultimate power must lie in the body which not only represents the people in some loose or metaphorical sense, but
has now been *elected* on the basis of universal suffrage,
namely the House of Commons. What this answer illustrates is that constitutional theory is a blend of law and
political theory. Nowhere is it clearly stated as a legal
principle that Parliament must be representative, and
indeed neither the Queen nor the Lords are, but no one
today could reasonably deny that in the last analysis it is
the fact of election which gives Parliament its authority,
and that the non-elected parts have authority ultimately
on the sufferance of the elected part, and not vice versa
(this was decided conclusively in January 1649)!

However, some people – and again, particularly those
desperate to block Brexit – would respond, 'Yes, but
once elected the members have the right to use their own
personal judgement', and they might mutter something
about Edmund Burke's Speech to the Electors of Bristol
in 1774, in which Burke proclaimed his right, if elected,
to do just that. But what is often forgotten is that the
Burkean view was always contestable, and indeed ran
flatly counter to long-standing practices in the England of
his day. It was not at all uncommon for MPs to be given

a mandate by the same assembly which had just elected them. One should remember that prior to the introduction of the secret ballot in 1872, elections took place in raucous public meetings – a good picture of them is to be found in George Eliot's relatively neglected novel *Felix Holt the Radical* – and the meetings could quite easily agree on instructions to be given to the members on how to vote in Parliament. This had indeed been the usual practice in Bristol (which had one of the most extensive franchises in pre-Reform Act England), and Burke's opponent in 1774 promised to continue the old custom; when Burke failed to do as his constituents wanted, he was promptly ejected at the next election.

It is not clear when the practice of local mandation ended, but by the late nineteenth century it had been replaced by the idea that a party manifesto serves as a mandate to the members elected under the banner of the party, an idea expressed most clearly in Baldwin's plea to the electors in the 1929 Conservative manifesto to give the government 'a national mandate' to pursue the policies set out in the manifesto. But the most important example of the way the idea of a national mandate in a manifesto functioned is to be found in the last major change in the functioning of Parliament, when the House of Lords had to come to terms with the radical programme of the Attlee government in 1945. Despite a large Conservative majority in the Lords, the Labour and Conservative leaders agreed that the House would not exercise its right under the 1911 Parliament Act to delay legislation for up to two years (what was later known as 'the Salisbury Compromise').

Defending the agreement, Lord Cranborne (to be Lord Salisbury after his father's death in 1947) said in August 1945:

> Whatever our personal views, we should frankly recognize that these proposals were put before the country at the recent General Election and that the people of this country,

with full knowledge of these proposals, returned the Labour Party to power. The Government may, therefore, I think, fairly claim that they have a mandate to introduce these proposals. I believe that it would be constitutionally wrong, when the country has so recently expressed its view, for this House to oppose proposals which have been definitely put before the electorate.[43]

He put it even more clearly in October:

If the country is behind [the government], their mandate will be renewed. If the country votes against them, it is clear that their policy is not approved. That is the proper constitutional course ... First, there is the Government: over them comes the authority of Parliament: and over Parliament the authority of the British people. That is the structure of the British Constitution. If the Government are hampered in their work, they can always go back to the sovereign people of this country from which Parliament gets its authority. But what is entirely contrary to the spirit of the Constitution is to attempt to stifle the free decisions of Parliament.[44]

Over Parliament is the authority of the British people. This was the implicit doctrine of the mandate: a policy which had been put before the electorate in the formal setting of a manifesto had a special authority, special enough to change a fundamental part of the British Constitution. By recognising this, Lord Salisbury (it is not far-fetched to say) preserved the House of Lords, and may also have preserved civil peace in an almost revolutionary moment. If the idea of a mandate had been rejected, Salisbury could not have done this: the Attlee government needed some means of enforcing the popular will against existing Parliamentary norms, and the obvious recourse was to the notion of a mandate. But the notion applies as much to the Lower as to the Upper House, and, as I said, it had traditionally been used to control members of the Commons.

The other weapon Attlee used against the House of Lords, as we have all been reminded recently, was prorogation. He used it in 1949 to create a special short session of Parliament to fulfil the requirements of the 1911 Act and force through a reduction of the Lords' delaying power to one year in the face of their hostility to the nationalisation of the steel industry. No one thought this particularly unconstitutional, and Salisbury once again acknowledged that they were bound by the 1945 general election mandate not to resist steel nationalisation.

It has been argued that the coming of life peers has changed the situation, since the Lords are now in some sense responsive to the needs of the country. But anyone who looks at the ranks of placemen in the modern chamber, and the cultural gulf between the members of the Lords and the wider population, would find this hard to believe: the modern Lords are as far out of line with the electorate as the hereditaries were, or maybe even more. If Salisbury's arguments were correct in 1945, they are equally correct today.

It has also occasionally been argued that manifestos should no longer be taken seriously; for example, an article in *The Economist* in 1997 remarked that a manifesto merely 'represents the terms of a truce between the factions that are inevitably present in any political party. The cost of these commitments, however, is that the government gets nailed down on policies which, even if they make sense at the time, may cease to make sense with passage of time.'[45] But this was completely and characteristically to miss the point. The manifesto is a mandate not because of the intrinsic qualities of the policies, but because it is the means by which electors can authorise a policy as well as authorising a set of representatives, just as their predecessors did in the days before the modern party manifesto. Common sense would tell us, and certainly told our predecessors, that representatives may prove unworthy of the trust we place in them, and five years is a long time to wait to repair any damage. Mandation ensured at least a measure of continued control, even though *The Economist* might view such a thing with distaste. 'Nailing down' is the *point*, not a defect.

The present Parliament has had two separate mandates to do with Brexit. Though this has been relatively neglected, it does have the traditional mandate of an election manifesto. The Conservatives' manifesto of 2017 contained a number of pledges about Brexit. First, it pledged that the referendum result would be respected: 'Following the historic referendum on 23rd June 2016, the United Kingdom is leaving the European Union.' Second, it ruled out continued membership of the single market and the customs union: 'As we leave the European Union, we will no longer be members of the single market or customs union but we will seek a deep and special partnership including a comprehensive free trade and customs agreement.' And third (something almost entirely ignored) it committed a Conservative administration to a specific negotiating framework with the EU: 'We believe it is necessary to agree the terms of our future partnership alongside our withdrawal, reaching agreement on both within the two years allowed by Article 50 of the Treaty on European Union.' As we all know, this last commitment was almost immediately torn up by May in the face of the EU's intransigence, a surrender which should have warned us about the fragility of the other manifesto commitments. The fact that May has presided over a minority government is irrelevant from the point of view of the mandate, since each Conservative MP was elected on this manifesto, and it is Conservative rebels who have largely been responsible for the long delay in implementing the referendum result.

The Labour manifesto was more evasive, but it too contained the blunt statement 'Labour accepts the referendum result', and it also contained various pledges to negotiate new free-trade agreements with other countries which would be incompatible with continued membership of the customs union. The DUP also proclaimed its absolute commitment to the result: 'The DUP believes that this decision must be upheld and our MPs fought against those who sought to overturn the people's decision, block Article 50 and tie the government's negotiation stance.' Unsurprisingly, neither the SNP nor Plaid Cymru committed themselves to respecting the referendum, and though the Liberal Democrats did do so, they did it in a very strange way, which, incidentally, seems to have popularised the term 'Hard Brexit':

> [W]e acknowledge the result of the 2016 referendum, which gave the government a mandate to start negotiations to leave. The decision Britain took, though, was simply whether to remain in or to leave the European Union. There was no option on the ballot paper to choose the shape of our future relationship with the EU on vital issues including trade, travel or security. While much remains uncertain about Theresa May's approach, it is now clear that the Conservatives are campaigning for a hard Brexit. This means leaving the single market, ending freedom of movement and abandoning the customs union – even though these choices will make the UK poorer and disappoint many leave voters who wanted a different outcome.

Since staying in the single market and the customs union *is* staying in the EU, for the EU is nothing more than these two arrangements, this form of words was particularly deceptive, but mysteriously it has become mainstream for all the minority parties in Parliament, other than the DUP.

So even on the traditional view of manifestos, a majority of sitting members of Parliament are mandated to leave the EU, understood as leaving the single market and the customs union. But the 2016 referendum was also in itself a mandate, of an extremely clear kind. Just as the Salisbury Compromise had force because it recognised a political reality – the power of a modern democratic vote – despite the fact that in strict law manifestos had no special significance, so the power of the vote in June 2016 has created a mandate for Parliament, despite the fact that in strict law it was only advisory. It was not merely an opinion poll, any more than a general election is merely an opinion poll on the policies put forward by the parties. The referendum was organised by the state, it gave everyone a vote, and there was a public understanding that the result would be respected. This was no less true of the referendum than of a party manifesto, and the referendum result in fact had additional authority, given by the fact that the proposition in the referendum was detached from other commitments and was the object of (for all its faults) an extensive and focused debate, comparable to the occasions in our past when a government has gone to the country seeking a mandate on a specific and crucial policy.

As I said, the programme of the Attlee government, though nostalgia has softened it, was close to revolutionary, and was denounced as such by the Conservatives. But rather than fight the programme through Parliamentary techni-calities, they chose to accept the reality of a democratic vote, conscious that not to do so would be both a major change in the real British Constitution, and a declaration of civil war. Far more was changed in Britain by the Attlee government than could possibly be changed by any form of Brexit, yet modern Parliamentarians seem incapable of emulating the wisdom of their precursors and recog-nising that above them is still 'the sovereign people of this country from which Parliament gets its authority'.

31 October 2019

On 23 July Boris Johnson was declared the new leader of the Conservative Party, gaining two-thirds of the members' votes, and he became Prime Minister the following day. He had campaigned on a platform of No Deal if necessary, but preferably a revised Withdrawal Agreement, and had committed himself to Brexit on 31 October. A struggle then began between Johnson's government and a hostile House of Commons. At the end of August Johnson advised the Queen to prorogue Parliament from the second week of September (in the event, 10 September) until 14 October. However, when Parliament met after the summer recess on 3 September, the Conservative MP Oliver Letwin tabled a motion to allow the Commons to go through all the stages of a backbench bill on the following day. Twenty-one Conservative MPs voted in favour of the motion and had the whip removed, leaving the government clearly without a majority. On 4 September the Commons duly passed Hilary Benn's European Union (Withdrawal) (No. 6) Bill. This obliged the Prime Minister to seek an extension from the European Council if by 19 October the House had not given its consent either to a withdrawal agreement or to leaving without a deal. It also named 31 January 2020 as a new withdrawal date which the Prime Minister was obliged to accept if it was offered by the European Council.

On 24 September the Supreme Court ruled that the prorogation had been illegal, and Parliament reconvened on 25 September. A week later Johnson outlined his new deal which had been agreed with the EU, replacing the 'Irish backstop' with an arrangement whereby Northern Ireland would now be treated differently from the rest of the UK. It would in effect remain in the single market, as it would have regulatory alignment with the Republic of Ireland, but it would leave the EU customs union. There would therefore in principle be regulatory checks but no customs checks between Britain and Northern Ireland, and customs checks but no regulatory checks between Northern Ireland and the Republic. The DUP refused to countenance this and withdrew their support for Johnson's Brexit policy. An attempt to get the deal accepted by the Commons on 19 October was blocked by an amendment tabled by Letwin requiring that implementation legislation be passed first; Johnson wrote to the European Council later that day, in accordance with the 'Benn Act', to ask for an extension. On 21 October Johnson introduced his European Union (Withdrawal Agreement) Bill, which received a second reading the next day, but was paused when the timetable motion was defeated. An extension to 31 January was agreed with the EU on 28 October, but the government (with Lib Dem and SNP support) succeeded on 30 October in passing an Early Parliamentary General Election Bill which nullified the effects of the Fixed-Term Parliaments Act. A general election was then called for 12 December.

As we enter upon the campaign for the general election, much of what I have said in the preceding essays remains depressingly relevant. The first and most important thing I said is that British politics since the 1970s has been subjected to a steady process of what one might call 'constitutional-ising', of which British membership of the EU has been the first and greatest example. There were, however, at least two other major instances: firstly, the UK's membership of the European Convention on Human Rights (ECHR); secondly, Blair's creation of a new 'Supreme Court' in 2005. These two are in fact closely connected, since it was the Blair government's alarm at a series of judgments from the European Court of Human Rights (ECtHR) which led to the creation of the Supreme Court.

In these judgments (many actually to do with UK cases) the ECtHR put forward the doctrine of the 'objective' independence and impartiality of tribunals, meaning by this that there should be no *appearance* of anything other than independence. The government feared that this might mean in the future that all the judgments of the then highest court in the UK, the Appellate Committee of the House of Lords, would be nullified by the ECtHR, since the Committee, being technically in the House of Lords, did not 'appear' to be independent of the legislature. This was despite the fact that, as the government admitted at the time, no one had ever accused the Committee of dependence on the Lords, and despite the fact that the ECtHR talked only about 'legitimate' doubts over judicial independence. A strong case could have been made that no legitimate doubts could be raised about the Committee, but one suspects that Blair was keen to use this pretext in order to 'modernise' the British constitution.

We now know the result of this, since one of the most striking episodes in the Brexit debate occurred in September when the Supreme Court ruled that 'Parliament', by which it appears to have meant the two Houses (or perhaps really the Commons), could not be prorogued by an 'executive' acting outside it unless good reasons could be given why the prorogation should take place – reasons, that is, which count as 'good' to the Court. It took its role to be exactly what had been assigned to it in the Act of 2005; namely, to be independent of both 'legislature' and 'executive' and to pronounce on their relationship, like the US Supreme Court (which the UK justices no doubt envy). Despite the Court's fondness in its judgment for citing Stuart cases, the justices forgot what the greatest seventeenth-century jurist,

Sir Matthew Hale, said during a struggle in 1675–6 over where ultimate appellate jurisdiction lay:

> the supreme court of this kingdom is neither the house of lords alone, nor the house of commons alone; no, nor both houses without the king. The high court of parliament, consisting of the king and both houses, is the supreme and only court of this kingdom, from which there is no appeal. Wherever the *dernier resort* is, there must needs be the sovereignty...[46]

But we must understand that this judgment of the Supreme Court is straightforwardly the consequence of the decision by British governments to sign up to the ECtHR and permit its judgments to overrule those of British courts. As I said in my essay on the ILO (11 April 2018), when the prospect of this happening first appeared, under the Attlee government, the Cabinet reacted very fiercely: 'It was intolerable that the code of common law and statute law which had been built up in this country over many years should be made subject to review by an International Court administering no defined system of law.'[47] But once the British had reluctantly accepted this principle, the door was opened for September's startling judgment in *R (on the application of Miller) (Appellant) v. The Prime Minister (Respondent)*.

The story is exactly the same as the story of the EU: a genuinely socialist government in Britain was determined to preserve the British constitution against the jurisdiction of an 'International Court administering no defined system of law', but subsequent governments were only too happy to let this happen. As I pointed out in my ILO essay, part of the Attlee government's resistance to the ECtHR was their fear that the clause guaranteeing rights of private property could be used to prevent nationalisation without, or with only minimal, compensation. They managed to get the clause modified and then signed up to the Convention, but forty years later the ECtHR adjudged that the compensation paid to shipbuilders when the Wilson government nationalised them had been insufficient, on the grounds that 'under the legal systems of the Contracting States, the taking of property in the public interest without payment of compensation is treated as justifiable only in exceptional circumstances not relevant for present purposes'.[48] This nullified all the work the Labour government had put in in 1951, and illustrates very well the dangers of 'no defined system of law'.

Although membership of the EU does not, strictly speaking, entail accession to the ECHR, the ECJ has agreed that it will use the Convention as indicative in its judgments, and the risk to the Appellate Committee came not merely through the ECHR but also through Britain's membership of the EU. Ironically enough, the ECJ has refused to countenance the EU's accession as a body to the Convention, despite this being written into the Lisbon Treaty as an intention, on the grounds that it would create a legal authority above the ECJ; the EU has proved much more sensitive in this regard than its member states, and it should perhaps be taken as a model by a post-Brexit UK!

The danger of constitutionalising, it should be reiterated, is that a constitution necessarily fossilises the cultural attitudes of the moment it was constructed, and in particular the cultural attitudes of the framers. This means that groups whose interests are still aligned in some way with the original intentions become privileged, since their interests cannot be challenged; because capitalism as a system meshes very neatly with (for example) a strong regime of private property, these kinds of modern constitutions inevitably tilt away from traditional Left policies. This may not matter if the constitution can easily be changed, but as we see in the US, even a constitution with a clearly defined and quite democratic method of amendment may become rigidified, with all sorts of adverse consequences (Citizens United...). And the EU Treaties are nothing like even the US constitution in this regard, since any alteration to them requires an astonishingly complex process, rendering (as I have said) the idea of 'Remain and Reform' ridiculous as a programme for the Left.

All this is pretty obvious, and was clear (as I have repeatedly pointed out) to the people on the Left who first scrutinised the institutions of post-war European union. Their far-sightedness has been vindicated by the virtual disappearance from the European political landscape of the old social democratic parties; it took a generation or so, but eventually the logic of the EU structures worked to reconfigure the politics of the continent. But why should the Left in Britain more recently have failed to see this, given that the real character of the institutions is still broadly what they were when they were originally created? For some in the Labour Party in the 1980s, as I have also said repeatedly, abandoning opposition to the EU provided the opportunity to lock the party into a post-Thatcher 'modernised' posture; but what has been really striking about the debate on the Left since 2016 has been the quite astonishing degree to which the kinds of facts which dominated the debates over the EEC from 1950 to 1975 have disappeared. The frivolity of the slogan 'Remain and Reform' is a prime example of this, but there are many others; the EU has been treated simply as a proxy for general political or cultural attitudes, rather than as an institution whose character should be analysed and assessed.

This might, paradoxically, be a reason for optimism, were it not that it is likely to have tragic consequences. I say this because the extreme reluctance on the part of the British Left – and indeed much of the British political class – to engage with the facts is to some degree testimony to a deep-seated conviction that in the end only Parliamentary politics matter. The Labour Party is full of people who airily dismiss any concerns about the way Parliament might be overridden in the future by European institutions: after all, Corbyn is apparently going to the country with a programme both of renationalisation of railways, utilities and the post office, and of (potentially) staying in the EU. Any manifesto commitments about nationalisation ought therefore to include the rider 'assuming we can get good lawyers to persuade the ECJ or the ECtHR that this is permitted, since the courts will decide whether we can do what we promise you we will do'. Good luck with that as an election-winning slogan. Dishonesty in this respect will, I am afraid, be baked into the manifesto. But it may not quite be dishonesty: as I said, it has proved very difficult to get the British out of their centuries-old confidence in the supremacy of Parliament and their familiarity with the business of Parliamentary politics. They do not understand that the world has changed about them, and those people on the Left who accuse their opponents of failing to understand the modern world are, ironically, even more guilty of this failing than their enemies.

But there is another and more depressing reason for the use of the EU as a proxy in a kind of culture war. Its institutions have induced a sense of powerlessness across the political divides, but different groups have reacted in different ways. For many Leave voters, it was immigration that made them realise for the first time what had happened, since they now saw a government having to negotiate – almost to plead – with the EU authorities in order to be able to control what used to be a familiar part of a state's business, the management of its borders. They responded, as we know, by demanding that they should be able to 'take back control'. But for many Remainers, their powerlessness had found a different kind of expression. Unable to envisage any new kind of politics, they had come to treat the EU as a kind of symbol, as inert in practice as a flag. To support the EU was to be a certain kind of person, and not to favour any specific policies, other than a vague kind of openness to the wider world. But here too their deep-seated Britishness revealed itself, since it is only vis-à-vis Britain that the EU represents open borders. For the rest of the world, as the dead at the bottom of the Mediterranean testify, it represents closed borders, except for the brief moment when Merkel in effect ordered them to be opened, a policy which was swiftly reversed when its consequences became clear.

This wholly expressive attitude to politics had as its almost necessary complement a refusal to think about alliances with the wrong kind of people. During the convulsion in British politics which (as many have observed) most resembles the Brexit debate, namely the struggle over the repeal of the Corn Laws, Marx praised the Chartists for precisely *not* refusing to ally with their enemies. As he said,

> [The working class] can and must accept the bourgeois revolutions as a precondition for the workers' revolution. However, they cannot for a moment regard it as their ultimate goal. That the workers really react in this way has been magnificently exemplified by the English Chartists in the most recent Anti-Corn Law League movement. Not for a moment did they believe the lies and inventions of the bourgeois radicals, not for a moment did they abandon the struggle against them, but quite consciously helped their enemies to victory over the Tories, and on the day after the abolition of the Corn Laws they were facing each other at the hustings, no longer Tories and free traders, but free traders and Chartists. And they won seats in parliament, in opposition to these bourgeois radicals.[49]

This could have been a model for the Left in the Brexit struggle, but this kind of long-term and tactical thinking proved to be beyond many of its leaders, largely, I think, because politics had become an arena for *display* and not *action*.

The oddity of British politics since the mid-1980s, as I stressed throughout these essays, was that Left and Right effectively swapped places over the EU. While the Left forgot its old objections, the Right forgot the old reasons why it had engineered Britain's accession in the first place – the desire to 'punch above our weight' in the post-imperial world, and the desire to neuter any future radical socialist policies through Britain's confinement in the legal order of a market. Some on the Right, it should be said, did not forget this, and May's 'deal', as quickly became apparent, was in fact an attempt to salvage the old Conservative vision of a Britain caught up in the legal regulations of the single market, while paying lip service to the referendum vote. It did this through the ingenious mechanism of the Northern Irish backstop, the practical consequence of which was to keep the whole of the UK in the single market and, arguably, the customs union, in order allegedly to maintain the integration of the market on the island of Ireland. Many people, including myself, in fact suspect that it was the other way round, and that the provisions about Ireland were really designed to bring about the desired result in Britain. May proclaimed her devotion to the Union, but as I observed in one of the essays (15 July 2018), the more she maintained a commitment to economic integration in Ireland, the more she provided an obvious template for an independent Scotland to seek a similar arrangement. As I said right at the beginning of this crisis, only a full Brexit is likely to slow down or even stop the slide towards Scottish independence, since only it introduces real costs to the process.

As we know, May's deal was defeated, and her time in office was cut short. The deal which Johnson has negotiated is quite different from hers, despite what some Brexiteers have alleged, since Johnson has abandoned May's device of leveraging Ireland to keep Britain effectively in the EU. Instead, he offers a reasonable version of what many supporters of Leave expected, and his proposed arrangement for Northern Ireland is not entirely unlike what David Grewal and I proposed (above, 19 November 2018), in that Northern Ireland ends up as a kind of special zone between Britain and the EU, though we envisaged it as something Britain could declare unilaterally and not as part of a deal. However, Johnson's deal means that – unlike with May's version – there is still all to play for. Though May's deal was ostensibly to do with a time-limited 'Withdrawal Agreement', the shape of the Agreement made it almost certain that it would not really be temporary: the basic structure of the future relationship between Britain and the EU was in fact quite precisely laid down in the Agreement, and from the point of view of the old pro-EU Tories there was no reason to change anything. They would simply have let matters drift and periodically renewed the Agreement, hoping that eventually Britain would go back in with little harm done. One could already hear the argument in 2025 or 2030: 'We should not put up with merely being rule-takers, we must play a full part in making the rules...'. This is not at all the case with Johnson's deal, precisely because it does not contain anything which could easily be extended into the future, unless Britain were simply to deal with the EU on so-called 'WTO terms'. It is extremely unlikely, however, that if Johnson wins the election he will be content with this; instead, he is almost certain to embark on negotiations for a long-term trade deal, the terms of which are at the moment utterly unclear. Anxiety about this presumably lay behind Nigel Farage's suspicion over Johnson's deal, and as so often in the recent past Farage's instincts may prove correct.

What, then, should the Left do? It is easy to say what it should have done. When I gave my lecture to Policy Exchange in July 2017 I was completely optimistic. In my eyes, the general election result vindicated what I had been saying: the British electorate, secure in the knowledge that Britain was about to leave the EU, were willing to take seriously a Labour Party with radical domestic policies, and were also abandoning the British equivalent of a far-right party. As I said, 'As in the 1930s, Britain may have dodged the bullet of a kind of fascism, and largely because its political structures once again *permit* rather than *constrain* radical politics.' It was even the case that the cause of Scottish nationalism seemed to be faltering. I did not then anticipate what was to happen, which was that the Labour Party failed to take advantage of Brexit. Its performance since then is largely what has landed us in the present mess, since if it had clearly accepted the result and used the opportunity to proclaim with conviction that it would occupy the new policy space which it opened up, many of the crises of the last two years could have been avoided. Its failure to do so was partly because of the general inability of the modern British Left to understand the issues about which their parents and grandparents had been extremely clear-headed, but partly because the leadership of the party was out-manoeuvred by the campaign for a second referendum, funded and managed by an assortment of former Blairites, and by Blair himself. This was a very subtle campaign, since it was able to insinuate that there were 'facts' about the break from the EU which had not been on people's minds at the time of the referendum, and which warranted a second look at the issue.

But as I observed in one of the essays (24 February 2019), these 'facts' were actually *artefacts*. If Blair and the others had accepted the result of the first referendum straight away, and had made it clear that there was now no alternative to leaving, then the long-drawn-out game of resisting 'No Deal' would not have happened. An EU faced with a united British ruling class would have had to offer something, and the vicious internecine struggles within both Left and Right could have been avoided. When Leavers during the referendum expressed optimism that if their side won then the new arrangements with the EU could be arrived at fairly easily (something for which they have widely been ridiculed), they did so in the expectation that the usual norms of British politics would hold, and that the result of a vote would be honoured. One of the few good things about the Supreme Court's judgment on prorogation, incidentally, was a throwaway remark implicitly endorsing this view. 'Technically, the result was not legally binding. But the Government had pledged to honour the result and it has since been treated as politically and democratically binding. Successive Governments and Parliament have acted on that basis' (para. 7).

However, for whatever reasons, the Labour Party was unable to go down the road which seemed to be wide open in July 2017. We will not know the result of the forthcoming general election until after this book is in press, but as things stand the outlook does not look very good in the immediate future for a Brexit which answers to the wishes of the Left. If Johnson wins decisively, the final deal will be on Conservative terms, while Corbyn and the timid Brexiteers around him are likely to lose their leadership of the Labour Party and be replaced by people more instinctively on the Remain side. If Corbyn wins, he has promised a weaker break from the EU than the Johnson deal, and conceivably no break at all. The most hopeful outcome, from my perspective, would be a narrow majority for Johnson, followed by the enactment of his Withdrawal Agreement and an abortive attempt at a more permanent arrangement, and a new election in which a Corbyn-led Labour Party could occupy the policy space that opens up after Brexit. But there are many things that could frustrate this outcome, not the least of which is the fact that many leading Labour politicians seem to have no desire to enter this space, and would prefer to put themselves forward merely as the managers of a liberal capitalism.

But that is the *immediate* future, and one of the things that has to be emphasised about Brexit is that its effects on British politics are going to be *long-term*. The logic of our new constitutional position after 1973–5 was not fully understood for a generation, while even its more narrowly political effects did not become evident until ten years later, when the Labour Party renounced its opposition to the EEC. There is every reason to think that the reverse process will take just as long.

Notes

1 'French President Charles DeGaulle's Veto on British Membership of the EEC, 14 January 1963', at https://www.files.ethz.ch/isn/125401/1168_DeGaulleVeto.pdf.

2 Quoted in Helen Parr, *Britain's Policy Towards the European Community: Harold Wilson and Britain's World Role, 1964–1967* (Abingdon: Routledge, 2006), p. 19.

3 Kevin D. Williamson, 'Chaos in the Family, Chaos in the State: The White Working Class's Dysfunction', *National Review*, 17 March 2016.

4 Matthew Parris, 'Tories should turn their backs on Clacton', *The Times*, 6 September 2014.

5 Thomas Frank, *Listen, Liberal: Or, Whatever Happened to the Party of the People?* (New York: Metropolitan, 2016).

6 Richard Tuck, 'The Left Case for Brexit', *Dissent*, 6 June 2016.

7 European Trade Union Confederation, *Trade Unions and Free Movement of Workers in the European Union* (April 2010), p. 5, https://www.etuc.org/sites/default/files/TURKISH_8_1.pdf.

8 House of Commons Library briefing paper no. 06091, 13 April 2016, p. 14.

9 It can be viewed at www.youtube.com/watch?v=ErAHSGY8W3c. The Rt. Hon. Caroline Flint's response

to my lecture can be viewed at www.carolineflint.org/the_left_and_brexit_my_speech_at_policy_exchange.

10 Henry Dunckley, *Lord Melbourne* (London, 1890), p. 167.

11 See in particular Wolfgang Streeck, *How Will Capitalism End?* (London: Verso, 2016), *Buying Time* (London: Verso, 2014) and *Politics in the Age of Austerity* (Cambridge: Polity, 2013), and the articles by Streeck, Jürgen Habermas, Etienne Balibar and Maurizio Ferrara in *Constellations* 21 (2014), pp. 199–228; Yanis Varoufakis, *And the Weak Suffer What They Must* (London: Bodley Head, 2016) and *Adults in the Room* (Bodley Head, 2017); Chris Bickerton, *The European Union: A Citizen's Guide* (London: Pelican, 2016).

12 Charles Moore, 'Reasoned democracy, not slinking back to the EU, is a much better antidote to Jeremy Corbyn', *The Telegraph*, 30 June 2017.

13 Richard Crossman, *The Diaries of a Cabinet Minister* (Hamish Hamilton and Jonathan Cape, 1976), 2 vols, II, p. 83.

14 Crossman, *Diaries*, II, p. 335.

15 Parr, *Britain's Policy Towards the European Community*, p. 20. This is a definitive work on the subject, and should be compulsory reading for everyone taking part in the current debate.

16 Crossman, *Diaries*, II, p. 83.

17 Karl Marx and Friedrich Engels, *Manifesto of the Communist Party*, in *Collected Works*, vol. 6 (London: Lawrence & Wishart, 2010), p. 488.

18 Thomas Piketty, *Capital in the Twenty-First Century* (Cambridge, MA: Harvard University Press, 2014).

19 EFTA, Judgment of the Court, 19 April 2016, https://eftacourt.int/wp-content/uploads/2019/01/14_15_Judgment_EN.pdf.

20 Moore, 'Reasoned democracy'.

21 See the extremely helpful briefing paper by Federico Mor, *EU State Aid Rules and WTO Subsidies Agreement*, House of Commons briefing paper no. 06775, 9 June 2017.

22 Philip Schofield, Catherine Pease-Watkin and Cyprian Blamires (eds), *The Collected Works of Jeremy Bentham: Rights, Representation, and Reform: Nonsense upon Stilts and Other Writings on the French Revolution* (Oxford: Oxford University Press, 2002), p. 272.

23 James T. Shotwell, ed., *The Origins of the International Labor Organization* (New York: Columbia University Press, 1934), 2 vols, I, p. 65.

24 The German willingness to consider these possibilities in October 1917 was presumably partly a response to America's entry into the war in April. Max Weber, for one, immediately saw that this meant the end of Germany's ambitions, despite its total victory in the East. The German section of the International Association for Labour Legislation was constituted by the Gesellschaft für soziale Reform, to which Weber and many of his associates such as Ernst Francke belonged, and the Gesellschaft produced an important paper drafted by Franke for the German government on the post-war labour settlement. See Shotwell, *The Origins*, II, pp. 50–1.

25 Shotwell, *The Origins*, II, p. 23. The Berne Resolutions read '(a) The enactment of prohibitions of emigration shall not be permissible. (b) The enactment of general prohibitions of immigration shall not be permissible' (II, p. 44).

26 The Leeds Resolutions, for example, proposed that 'there should be in every country a special commission on emigration and immigration, consisting of representatives of the government and of the organizations of employers and workers of the country. The recruiting of workmen in a foreign country should only be permitted if the commissions of the interested countries whose duty it is to examine into the question as to whether the demand for, and the extent of, such a recruiting really corresponds with the needs of an industry or district ... [*sic*: something missing in Stockwell text]'; they also added, 'Should the need arise to employ colored labor, the recruiting must proceed under the same conditions as apply to European workmen' (Shotwell, *The Origins*, II, p. 24).

27 Article 414 allowed a Commission of Enquiry authorised by the ILO to indicate in its report 'the measures, if any, of an economic character against a defaulting Government which it considers to be appropriate, and which it considers other Governments would be justified in adopting', measures which could be confirmed by the Permanent Court of International Justice. The initial British draft included the proposition that 'Any State, therefore, which does not carry

out a Convention designed to prevent oppressive conditions is guilty of manufacturing under conditions which create a state of unfair competition in the international market. The appropriate penalty accordingly appears to be that when a two-thirds majority of the Conference is satisfied that the terms of the Convention have not been carried out the signatory States should discriminate against the articles produced under the conditions of unfair competition proved to exist unless those conditions were remedied within one year or such longer period as the Conference might decide' (Shotwell, *The Origins*, II, p. 125). The British negotiator Edward Phelan, in one of his contributions to Volume I, described this as 'a somewhat daring but interesting suggestion' (I, p. 118). A later amendment gave the ILO authority to decide what kind of action should be taken. It should be said that this procedure has only once been invoked, when sanctions were applied against Myanmar in 2000 for violating Convention 029, against forced labour. See ILO, *Record of Proceedings 101st Session*, 15 May 2012, PR No. 2-1.

28 C026, Minimum Wage-Fixing Machinery Convention 1928, denounced July 1985; C094 Labour Clauses (Public Contracts) Convention 1949, denounced September 1982; and C095, Protection of Wages Convention 1949, denounced September 1983.

29 Shotwell, *The Origins*, I, p. 246.

30 Marco Duranti, *The Conservative Human Rights Revolution: European Identity, Transnational Politics, and the Origins of the European Convention* (Oxford: Oxford University Press, 2017).

31 Duranti, *The Conservative Human Rights Revolution*, pp. 103, 105.

32 Duranti, *The Conservative Human Rights Revolution*, p. 220. Duranti observes persuasively that this resembled the views and the language of Hayek's *The Road to Serfdom*, which also argued for the creation of a supranational authority 'which effectively limits the powers of the state over the individual' (p. 222). The future Lord Hailsham also said something similar in the Commons in 1949, foreshadowing his famous attack on 'an elective dictatorship' in 1976.

33 Duranti, *The Conservative Human Rights Revolution*, p. 247.

34 National Archives CAB 128.18, formerly CM 52 (50), p. 191.

35 Roger Broad, *Labour's European Dilemmas: From Bevin to Blair* (Basingstoke: Palgrave Macmillan, 2001), p. 60.

36 Quoted in Michael Newman, 'The British Labour Party', in Richard T. Griffiths, ed., *Socialist Parties and the Question of Europe in the 1950s* (Leiden: E. J. Brill, 1993), p. 165.

37 Nye Bevan, 'Back to Free Markets and the Jungle', *Tribune*, 30 August 1957.

38 On 21 June 2018 Airbus published a 'risk assessment' in which they stated that Britain leaving without a deal 'would force Airbus to reconsider its investments in the UK, and its long-term footprint in the country'.

39 National Archives CAB 129/102/7, formerly C (60) 107, p. 9.

40 National Archives CAB 129/102/7, formerly C (60) 107, p. 3.

41 It is sometimes said that Britain could solve the 'problem' of the Irish border by invoking Article XXIV.3, which allows countries to make special arrangements to facilitate frontier traffic. But this is a much more limited provision than Article XXI, and would not (for example) allow the whole of Northern Ireland to be treated as a frontier zone.

42 National Archives CAB 129/102/7, formerly C (60) 107, p. 6.

43 HL Hansard, 16 August 1945, vol. 137, col. 47

44 HL Hansard, 31 October 1945, vol. 137, col. 613.

45 'A Burning Issue: Party Manifestos', *The Economist*, 25 January 1997.

46 *The Jurisdiction of the Lords House, or Parliament, Considered According to Antient Records*, ed. Francis Hargrave (London, 1796), p. 205. Hale was an acquaintance of Hobbes, and though often a critic of him, in this respect he agreed that the power of interpretation cannot ultimately be separated from the power of legislation.

47 National Archives CAB 128.18, formerly CM 52 (50), p. 191.

48 *Lithgow and Others v. The United Kingdom* (1986), para. 120.

49 Karl Marx, 'Moralising Criticism and Critical Morality' (1847), in Karl Marx and Friedrich Engels, *Collected Works*, vol. 6 (London: Lawrence and Wishart, 1976), p. 333.